Praise for Grow Strong Character

"As a leader with decades of experience at the helm of WD-40 Company, I wholeheartedly endorse ***Grow Strong Character***. This book is a masterful guide to developing the 36 essential character skills needed for personal and professional success. Filled with insightful anecdotes, actionable advice, and powerful quotes, it offers a practical roadmap for leaders at all levels. Dr. Coates' emphasis on self-awareness, self-discipline, and resilience aligns with my own experiences, making this book an invaluable resource for anyone committed to excellence."

—**Garry Ridge,** Chairman Emeritus WD-40 Company, The Culture Coach

"***Grow Strong Character*** is a must-read for leaders at any stage. It's packed with practical tools for understanding your strengths and weaknesses, growing through adversity, and boosting your emotional intelligence. This book isn't just for leaders—it offers something valuable for everyone, helping you build a stronger character and become more resilient and self-aware in all areas of life."

—**Damon Lembi,** CEO of Learnit & Author of *The Learn-It-All Leader*

"This book tackles the most foundational aspect of leadership—character strength. What I particularly appreciated about it, though, is the highly practical lens that it covers the topic through—from the short chapters that can be read independently and referenced at a later time, to the "why" to internalize the necessity of a particular skill, or the specific actions one can use as a starting point to improve. A worthwhile read for anyone on their leadership journey —whether starting or seasoned."

—**Omar Halabieh,** Head of Technology, Amazon Payment Services

"A practical, achievable, empowering guide that defines what each critical character skill is, why it's important, and ways we can strengthen it. On behalf of myself and every human that I have or will have a relationship with, *Thank you.*"

—**Kristin Ford Hinrichs,** Chief Effectiveness Officer, Best in Learning

"Drawing from decades of lived experience, Dr. Coates shares invaluable insights into human character development. His clear and engaging format offers inspiration, compelling stories, concise definitions, and practical actions to integrate each character trait into our lives. This book is both comprehensive and profoundly useful, serving as an essential guide for people at every stage of life. It's a true handbook for living one's life to the fullest, and recognizing the character of others."

—**Dan Kent,** Business & Executive Coach

"One of the things I absolutely love about ***Grow Strong Character*** is how Dr. Coates facilitates the reader's understanding and development of the 36 Character skills. Each chapter identifies the skill, provides a short story example, and then briefly explains what the skill is all about and why it is important, followed by actions one can take to improve or develop the skill. I can see this book being useful for young people just starting out in their careers, as well as for high-potential employees, individual contributors, managers, and leaders who want to develop strong character."

—**Nicholas J. Scalzo, Ed.D.,** President, OnTrack Training LLC

"No matter how well you may believe you have mastered a specific skill, Dr. Coates always seems to have a question or perspective that makes you re-examine that belief! And more often than not, your knowledge and skill are enhanced by his greater understanding. The 36 core character skills identified in this excellent book can help you achieve and reach the optimum you.

"I have known and respected the author's work for more than 25 years, and I feel that having read this book I know him a little better. And what's more, I know more about myself, the skills I have, and those I need to enhance further to become the authentic leader of others, as well as myself."

—**Graham Da Costa,** CEO, Shine Feedback Ltd

"If you were to ask a former boss or friend to provide a character reference for you as you apply for a new job, what would it look like? Dr. Coates provides a comprehensive review of 36 Character Skills, many of which I'm sure you would want to see included. Charting this course of professional development is not easy without a guide. Now you have it."

—**Rick Stamm,** founder, The TEAM Approach, Inc.

Grow Strong Character

Other Books by Dennis E. Coates, Ph.D.

For Business

Connect With Your Team: Mastering the Top 10 Communication Skills (with Meredith M. Bell)

Peer Coaching Made Simple: How to Do the 6 Things That Matter Most When Helping Someone Improve a Skill

The Dark Secret of HRD: Four Things You Need to Know to Stop Wasting Money on Training

For Parents

The Truth about Distracted Driving: 10 Ways to Save Your Teen Driver's Life (and Possibly Your Own)

Connect with Your Kid: Mastering the Top 10 Parent-Child Communication Skills

Parents Coaching Parents: How Parents Can Help Each Other Improve Family Communication Skills

How Your Teen Can Grow a Smarter Brain: 7 Game-Changers That Will Maximize Your Teen's Brainpower—Permanently, 2nd Edition

Preparing Your Teen for Life: 50 Insights to Help Your Child Grow Up Happy, Successful, and Independent

The Sacred Purpose: How Youth Sports Organizations Can Do More to Prepare Athletes for Life

Conversations with the Wise Uncle: The Secret to Being Strong as a Teenager and Preparing for Success as an Adult

Conversations with the Wise Aunt: The Secret to Being Strong as a Teenager and Preparing for Success as an Adult

Grow Strong Character

A Guide for Developing 36 Character Skills to Achieve Excellence in Every Area of Your Life

Dennis E. Coates, Ph.D.

First Summit Publishing

Grow Strong Character: A Guide for Developing 36 Character Skills to Achieve Excellence in Every Area of Your Life

Printed in the United States of America
First Summit Publishing
An imprint of Performance Support Systems, Inc.
757-873-3700

Cover and book design: Paula Schlauch

ISBN: 978-0-9850156-4-0

Quantity sales. Special discounts are available on quantity purchases by corporations, associations, and others. For details, contact us at support@growstrongleaders.com or 757-656-4765.

Contents

Introduction

Many organizations prioritize growing strong leaders. Leadership requires many essential skills, so evolving as a leader is a never-ending process. Even top executives invest in coaching for their leadership development. While a successful program may begin in the classroom with introductions to basic concepts and skills, this kind of information needs to be followed by a much more critical phase: a long-term process of on-the-job skill application and coaching for three major skill-building areas.

One classic area of leader development includes basic skills such as teambuilding, delegating, empowering, problem-solving, decision-making, planning, supervising, managing performance, managing time, and leading meetings. Most leader development programs focus on these traditional topics.

However, effective communication is the most crucial leadership skill and enables vital person-to-person interactions. It's impossible to create high-performing teams without effective leader-team communication. The skills include listening to understand, asking questions that get people to think, guiding learning from experience, getting buy-in for expectations, offering encouragement, expressing appreciation, giving feedback constructively, accepting feedback graciously, engaging in dialogue, and resolving conflict creatively. The how-to book ***Connect with Your Team*** describes these skills in detail.

The third major area of leader development is the focus of this book: ***Grow Strong Character***. The 36 character skills it describes are work habits—behavior patterns that help a leader do the hard, effective, and right things when dealing with the many leadership challenges. We refer to character strengths as skills because they're behavior patterns. Like other skills, such as those needed for technical work, sports, arts, thinking, and communicating with others, these are habits you can develop and continuously improve throughout a lifetime. You develop them by practicing and repeating them so often that the brain cells that enable the actions are stimulated to interconnect physically into a circuit. When these brain circuits are finally established, using the skills becomes your automatic response, the way you typically approach your work—and life. They become a part of who you are: *your character*.

The skills that comprise character strength are a significant aspect of *emotional intelligence*. This book organizes them into three categories:

- Building a stronger self
- Building stronger relationships
- Building a stronger work ethic

Scan the "Contents" page and some chapters to familiarize yourself with the book. You'll see that the chapters are always brief. They begin with an anecdote or two to illustrate the particular skill. Most of these stories come from my experiences dealing with challenges. The chapters then define the skill and describe its importance. You'll also see quite a few quotes from well-known people because character skills were involved in their achievements. Hopefully, what they have to say will inspire and encourage you. Most important are the recommendations for implementing each skill—ideas for the repeated practice you'll need to establish the skill.

The most effective approach to skill development is to focus: practice one skill at a time, or at most, two related skills. While each chapter is an excellent introduction to one of the skills, it would be a mistake to stop there. Strengthening a behavior pattern requires more than knowing what to do. It takes lots of doing—many repetitions over time, during the course of work, to establish the kind of automatic behavior pattern that will consistently serve you in your busy life.

For example, if you want ideas for strengthening your compassion, go to Chapter 18, which is a basic introduction to that skill, including many suggested activities for practicing compassion. By focusing on this one skill and implementing some of the suggested developmental activities, you can learn from your experiences as you work on making the skill a permanent behavior pattern.

One final tip. It will significantly accelerate your growth if you partner with someone who cares about your success. Ideally, this person is someone else working on building character strength. But it could also be your boss, an internal learning and development staff member, a consultant, a mentor, or a spouse. Commit to contacting each other regularly to discuss your attempts and what you learned from them. Most important, to get encouragement. Because once you start consciously working on character skills, you'll discover that if you want to improve who you are in any area of strong character, the learning journey will involve both successes and frustrations, so you'll need to stick with it. To give you and your coaching partner the confidence to be helpful, you can get tips for using skills you already have in the brief book, ***Peer Coaching Made Simple***.

Grow Strong Character is one of the resources that support participants in the ***GSL Skillbuilder*** program. Furthermore, the book is an excellent resource for anyone who wants to build strong character, even if they aren't involved in a formal leadership development program.

PART ONE

BUILDING A STRONGER SELF

Every adult knows that life is full of challenges, both large and small. Sometimes you can see them coming, others surprise you—every day, every week, throughout a lifetime. Knowledge, skill, and experience are powerful resources for dealing with these issues. But without character strength, which allows you to bring your best self to challenging situations, life can be difficult and disappointing. People who lack the strength to deal with the inevitable adversities can be beaten down by life. Burdened by failure, loss, despair, and even addiction, a precious life can become miserable.

The 12 skills listed below are the kind that enable you to attack a variety of situations and deal with any problem. In later sections, you can learn about character skills that help in relationships and at work.

1. Self-awareness
2. Self-development
3. Self-discipline
4. Self-confidence
5. Self-esteem
6. Humility
7. Optimism
8. Resilience
9. Rationality
10. Courage
11. Composure
12. Patience

"Knowing yourself is the beginning of all wisdom."

Aristotle, Greek philosopher

"An unexamined life is not worth living."

Socrates, Greek philosopher

"He who knows others is wise; he who knows himself is enlightened."

Lao Tzu, Chinese philosopher

"Feedback is the breakfast of champions."

Ken Blanchard, American author

1

Self-Awareness

Explore who you are, and you'll discover who you can become.

People are so complex that they can easily become a mystery to themselves. But it's an intriguing mystery. Self-discovery is an adventure, and the reward at the end is a greater understanding of who you are, giving you more control of your life. You can't control what you don't understand.

I'll never forget the first time we used 360-degree feedback software in our company. Reading my report gave me some helpful insights about my strengths. But I also learned about a behavior that had been causing problems. And I had no idea I was doing it.

Whenever I had an important point to make in meetings, I'd just speak up. I wasn't aware that I was interrupting people. As a result, they felt disrespected and even avoided contributing. After their feedback pointed this out, I apologized and promised to be patient, listen, and hold my thoughts until it was my turn to speak.

Getting this feedback reminded me that the people around me were already aware of my obvious strengths and weaknesses. I was the one with blind spots. I was lucky to have a mirror held up to my behavior so I could see myself as they saw me.

This feedback was a true gift because it increased my level of self-awareness.

What is SELF-AWARENESS?

Like all the people around you, you're a rich, one-of-a-kind combination of many aspects of being human: your feelings, thoughts, and memories; your values, preferences, beliefs, and biases; your desires, motivations, and goals; and your knowledge, skills, habits, strengths, and weaknesses.

Your awareness of these aspects of yourself depends on how willing you are to examine them in detail. Ask yourself questions such as:

- *What are my true feelings about this?*
- *Why do I want to do this?*
- *Why do I tend to do it this way?*
- *What's important to me?*

And so on. There's a lot to be aware of, so improving self-awareness could involve many efforts of self-discovery.

Why self-awareness is important:

Your ability to set goals, achieve them, and create a fulfilling life depends on how well you use your strengths and work around your weaknesses. And you can't do that without knowing what they are.

Whatever you try to do will be more difficult if you aren't self-aware. You need to know what you're capable of and what you're not. You need to know what's important to you. You need to know how you really feel about what you're doing. It's hard to make changes when you don't know what you should work on. Yet almost no one has perfect insight into their behavior. You can start by discovering how others see you. If you're lucky enough to get honest feedback and you sense they're trying to help, thank them and decide how to work on specific areas.

"Noticing a single shortcoming in ourselves is far more useful than seeing a thousand in someone else. When it is our own, we can correct it."

Dalai Lama, Tibetan religious leader

What you can do to strengthen your self-awareness:

- ✓ Keep a journal about your efforts to deepen your self-awareness.
- ✓ Practice regular meditation or deep introspection.
- ✓ Identify and clarify your values and guiding principles.
- ✓ Get in touch with real-time body sensations, such as tension, fatigue, or physical discomfort.
- ✓ Ask for feedback and accept it graciously.
- ✓ Reflect on how your behavior and communication impact others and identify a positive change you can make.
- ✓ Make rank-ordered lists:
- ✓ The ten most important things in your life
- ✓ Your top five personal goals
- ✓ Your strongest motivators
- ✓ Your five most significant strengths
- ✓ Areas of knowledge and skill you'd like to improve
- ✓ Your most strongly held beliefs
- ✓ Your favorite activities and why you enjoy each one

As you increase your self-awareness, you can gain in personal growth, self-acceptance, self-management, and decision-making. You can become more conscious of your strengths and use them more effectively. And as you make an effort to improve, your work will have better results. You'll take on challenges with greater confidence and resilience.

"What a great gift we would have if we could only see ourselves as others see us."

Robert Burns, Scottish poet

Be honest about your limitations, and you'll discover who you can become.

"If I had eight hours to chop down a tree, I'd spend six sharpening my ax."

Abraham Lincoln, American president

"Whatever we learn to do, we learn by actually doing it: men come to be builders, for instance, by building, and harp players by playing the harp. In the same way, by doing just acts, we come to be just; by doing self-controlled acts, we come to be self-controlled; and by doing brave acts, we become brave."

Aristotle, Greek philosopher

"Experience is not what happens to you. It is what you do with what happens to you."

Aldous Huxley, British novelist

"Live as if you were to die tomorrow. Learn as if you were to live forever."

Mohandas Gandhi, Indian political leader

2

Self-Development

You didn't get to choose your parents. But you can choose who their child will be.

Even if you're the kind of person who wants to grow stronger to meet the challenges of life, you'll have to make an effort to set aside time for learning in a day filled with work and family activities. And it may seem uncomfortable or daunting when you realize that learning something new may require you to let go of something you've learned in the past. But the benefits of ongoing self-development are enormous.

One of my colleagues is a person I consider to be a "life-long learner." I've known her for almost 50 years, and she's been a self-developer all those years. I remember a time when she had to have major surgery to correct a life-threatening condition. The procedure disrupted her hormonal system, which caused a chemical imbalance in her brain, leading to depression. Her doctors attacked the problem with medication, but it was trial and error to find the right combination of drugs, some of which were addictive. What my friend did was take the initiative to slowly reduce and eliminate the medications, while training her brain to approach life with a serene, positive outlook. This monumental effort to improve her condition took more than a year, and she learned some powerful skills along the way. In the end, it worked. She did for herself what her doctors could not do. Then she turned what she learned about healing into a business.

Today, she's also an accomplished business manager, a creative web designer, a book producer, a computer programmer, and a technical support specialist. And, oh yeah, a gardener and a mom to five cats.

Amazing.

I consider myself a lifelong learner, too. I received my Ph.D. when I was 32. I've learned almost everything I know now since then, and I'm still learning.

What is SELF-DEVELOPMENT?

Self-development is the ongoing process of improving yourself by striving for personal growth, fulfillment, and self-actualization. It could involve enriching your knowledge or building new skills, as well as improving your physical, emotional, intellectual, and spiritual well-being. In the best case, self-development is a lifelong journey, constantly focusing your internal motivation, self-discipline, and commitment to do the work.

Why self-development is important:

Our world is always changing, and the rate of change is accelerating. If you want to be successful, you'll need to continue adapting to it. That means more learning, growing, and changing. Through self-development, you can cultivate a more capable version of yourself. By continuously acquiring new knowledge, skills, and experience, you empower yourself to accomplish more toward a fulfilling and meaningful life.

"Still I am learning."

Michelangelo, Italian artist

What you can do to strengthen your self-development:

- ✓ Engage in self-assessment to help you understand your best opportunities for improvement.
- ✓ Set a specific, measurable, achievable, relevant, and time-bound goal to guide you toward a specific aspect of personal growth.
- ✓ Continue learning from experience. Analyze your successes and mistakes for lessons learned.
- ✓ Focus on improving your interpersonal communication skills, which will make a huge difference in all your relationships.
- ✓ Do more to take care of your physical, mental, and emotional well-being through exercise, healthy eating, and stress management.
- ✓ Actively seek opportunities for self-development through purposeful reading, workshops, seminars, conferences, and advanced education.
- ✓ Establish relationships with mentors, coaches, and people who are more accomplished than you are.
- ✓ Stay curious about all aspects of life. Be a seeker of wisdom.
- ✓ Don't wait for the course. Launch an effort of self-learning.
- ✓ Read a book in a new topic area.

With so many ways to get stronger, I recommend that you:

- Concentrate your efforts in one or two areas.
- Commit to stick with it.
- Set a goal to establish a habit of self-development.

- Ask someone to connect with you regularly to hold you accountable, talk with you about what you learned from your experiences, and encourage you.

"That which we persist in doing becomes easier—not that the nature of the task has changed, but our ability has increased."

Ralph Waldo Emerson, American philosopher

When you learn something new, that treasure will never be taken from you.

"Freedom is not procured by a full enjoyment of what is desired, but by controlling the desire."

Epictetus, Greek philosopher

"There is no such thing as a great talent without great willpower."

Honoré de Balzac, French novelist

"The undisciplined are slaves to moods, appetites, and passions."

Stephen Covey, American author

"The first and best victory is to conquer self."

Plato, Greek philosopher

3

Self-Discipline

If it's in your power to do it, it's in your power to not do it.

It takes grit to stay on track until you achieve the result you've been aiming for, especially when you could put it off and do something that's immediately satisfying. You need to say no to temptations, use your time wisely, and stick with a task until it's completed.

During the holiday season, what sometimes happens to me is what happens to millions of Americans—I gain more than 5 pounds. Parties, family gatherings, food, wine, football, basketball, snacks, and beer. Woo-hoo! If that isn't enough to drive me to a New Year's resolution, I don't know what is.

During that same period of time, a good friend of mine *lost* more than five pounds!

Not only that, but he had been on a steady weight-loss program for about two years, and he lost a total of 60 pounds. He went from 240 pounds to 180 pounds—very close to his goal weight.

Yes, millions of people lose weight every year, and many of them actually keep it off. That means I can do it, too. So can you. How my buddy did it can tell us a lot about self-discipline.

Back in 2002, he was motivated by the symptoms of Type II diabetes to sign up for the Weight Watchers program. You may know that Weight Watchers is a no-gimmick approach to losing weight. It involves diet, nutrition education, exercise, coaching, counting and recording "points" in a journal, and most of all, standing on a scale at the end of each week. Losing weight is actually a simple activity. You lose weight every day because you expend more calories than you intake in food. But you don't know whether you're doing that unless you measure and keep track.

Well, it worked. During that year, he lost 50 pounds in 9 months. When he achieved his goal and shifted to "maintenance," he felt he no longer needed to keep a record of his food intake. Also, he had a stressful job that caused him to snack more and exercise less. Slowly, he gained back all those 50 pounds—plus 10 more pounds. It's an old story.

But in 2007, he retired and resolved to make some permanent changes in his life. A diabetic at the age of 62 and with a history of heart disease in his family, he felt that if he didn't change his lifestyle, he could be risking his life. He wanted to exercise regularly and eat more sensibly. He signed up for Weight Watchers again, this time with renewed motivation. He wanted to reduce his medications. He wanted to be able to enjoy activities like hiking and SCUBA diving. His goal was to lose 60 pounds before 2010—and keep them off.

This time, he had more going for him than motivation. For one thing, the work-related stress in his life was gone, and he had more time for exercise. For another, he had the support of his wife, who participated in the program with him. Also, he had a great coach, the program director at their weekly Weight Watcher meetings.

In addition, my friend relied on self-discipline and perseverance. He quickly got back into the habit of measuring food and recording his intake. At the end of every day, he knew for sure whether he had burned more calories than he had taken in. He went to the gym five times a week. And when arthritis made it hard to put in time on the treadmill, he took up swimming.

Then something wonderful happened. He found that what he was doing had become a habit, which meant that doing all the right things wasn't so much a matter of willpower anymore. It was simply the way he lived his life. He had established new behavior patterns.

I asked him how he stayed on track during the holidays. He said that he considered parties and get-togethers "high-risk situations," which caused him to focus on self-discipline.

In short, he's a true Weight Watchers success story. This time he did "maintenance" right. He took the weight off slowly. He made permanent changes in his lifestyle.

What you should do is often at odds with what you want to do. You may need to lose weight, but you'd rather eat a big helping of your favorite ice cream. You may need to rake leaves, but you'd rather watch a football game. An important project sits idle on your desk, but it would be less stressful to read a magazine. It takes inner strength to say no to temptations, do what you need to do, use your time wisely, and stick with a task until it's completed.

What is SELF-DISCIPLINE?

Self-discipline involves staying focused on a specific result and steadily working toward a specific goal while maintaining standards of excellence. You achieve self-discipline by managing your thoughts, motivations, and behavior to avoid distractions and resist immediate gratification. You say no when it's in your best interests to do so.

Why self-discipline is important:

Challenging projects usually require a high level of commitment and self-discipline. You may be interrupted. You may get a phone call or an unexpected visitor. Your desire to do something else, perhaps something easier or more pleasant, can take you off task. Self-discipline is necessary for achieving any worthwhile project. Imagine what it takes to launch a new business, remodel a home, write a book, or create a marketing strategy from scratch and implement it. Projects like these require focus, making sacrifices, and relentless effort. Your success, your ultimate happiness—maybe even your life—could depend on it.

"There never has been, and cannot be, a good life without self-control."

Leo Tolstoy, Russian novelist

What you can do to strengthen your self-discipline:

- ✓ Set a specific achievable goal, along with realistic expectations for yourself.
- ✓ Concentrate on your highest priority task, and continuously maintain your focus despite distractions or difficulties.
- ✓ If your work involves lots of tasks, prioritize them. Then, identify the most important task, break it into manageable steps, get organized, and manage your time efficiently.
- ✓ Make sacrifices to resist the short-term allure of distractions and instead focus on finishing your current big project.
- ✓ Use your commitment and focus to avoid procrastination and do what's needed to achieve your goal.
- ✓ Consistently apply self-discipline to all aspects of your life, including work, relationships, health, fitness, and overall well-being.

✓ Practice managing interruptions and delaying gratification to finish a task.

✓ Use a polite, affirming way to say: "I'd like to do that later, but right now, it's important for me to finish what I'm doing."

✓ When tempted by a distraction, remind yourself how important your current task is.

Like improving any skill, strengthening your behavior patterns for self-discipline will take time and effort. As they say, *you gotta get your reps*. So, commit to exercising more self-control and stick with it. And I strongly recommend meeting regularly with someone who will hold you accountable, help you learn from your efforts, and encourage you.

"In reading the lives of great men, I found that the first victory they won was over themselves....self-discipline with all of them came first."

Harry Truman, American president

Make the best use of your time, and you'll always have enough.

"Believe and act as if it were impossible to fail."

Charles F. Kettering, American engineer

"There's a big difference between confidence and conceit. To me, conceit is bragging about yourself. Being confident means you believe you can get the job done."

Johnny Unitas, American professional football player

"No one knows what he can do until he tries."

Publilius Syrus, Roman author

"My mother taught me very early to believe I could achieve any accomplishment I wanted to. The first was to walk without braces."

Wilma Rudolph, American Olympic sprint champion

4

Self-Confidence

Believe you can or believe you can't. Either way, you'll prove yourself right.

Most people underestimate themselves. Because mistakes, shortfalls, and failures pepper every life, people tend to be more aware of their shortcomings and limitations than they are of their strengths and possibilities.

I once knew a woman who had a Master's degree in English from a well-known university. She loved fiction and poetry, and we would frequently talk about books. She often said that she would like to write a novel someday. One day, I encouraged her to take the first step by writing a story. To my surprise, she expressed reluctance, explaining that she wasn't ready to try it. I was puzzled by her attitude, because she was a student of literature and a thoughtful, intuitive person. I had seen examples of her writing. It was quite elegant—far above the norm. She simply believed that she couldn't do it. And so she never did.

By contrast, our company once hired a young computer programmer who declared that our new web-based program needed a content management system. I knew he had no experience with this kind of programming, but he claimed that not only could he do it, but he would also create a generic, self-customizable content management system that would become a product in its own right. So we gave him the project. He made a lot of mistakes along the way, but it was amazing to watch him learn. And in the end, he did what he said he would do, even though he'd never done anything like this before.

The difference between these two people is *self-confidence*, the belief that you can accomplish a difficult task.

It's easy to doubt yourself. You know you have certain strengths, and you've accomplished many things in your life. You may feel it's foolhardy not to recognize your limitations. Fine, but don't sell yourself short. You have know-how, imagination, and energy. You can build on what you already know, learning as you go. You can work hard and refuse to quit.

What is SELF-CONFIDENCE?

Healthy self-confidence means having an accurate assessment of your strengths. You have a realistic and positive perception of your knowledge, skills, talents, and potential. This belief in your capacity comes from experience, from taking on challenges, and achieving noteworthy results. Thus, you come to believe in your ability to solve problems, make good decisions, overcome obstacles, and achieve your goals.

Why self-confidence is important:

If you doubt your abilities, you aren't likely to take on tough challenges. Knowing what you're good at can make you assertive, bold, and resilient. You believe in your potential. Self-confidence influences ambition, prudent risk-taking, and perseverance. Strong self-confidence could lead to embracing new opportunities and making the most of your talents.

"Make the most of yourself by fanning the tiny, inner sparks of possibility into flames of achievement."

Golda Meir, Israeli prime minister

What you can do to strengthen your self-confidence:

- ✓ Make a list of your top skills.
- ✓ Acknowledge something hard you did successfully.
- ✓ When you complete a successful project or achieve a goal after a significant effort, give yourself credit. Tell yourself: *I did that.*
- ✓ When addressing a group or audience, come prepared, so you express your ideas convincingly, maintain eye contact, and project your voice with assurance.
- ✓ Consider other people's opinions, but trust your judgment. Make choices based on your own beliefs and values, taking responsibility for the outcomes.
- ✓ You matter. Express your needs, opinions, and boundaries assertively. Communicate your thoughts and feelings without hesitation.
- ✓ Set realistic goals for yourself and believe in your ability to achieve them.
- ✓ Based on a realistic assessment of your strengths, take on challenges, believing in your ability to overcome obstacles. See these situations as opportunities rather than as threats, and be willing to step out of your comfort zone.
- ✓ Welcome constructive feedback. Accept it graciously, evaluate it objectively, and use it to improve yourself.
- ✓ Exhibit positive body language, such as standing tall, making eye contact, and having relaxed and open gestures.
- ✓ Create the three lists of the self-confident individual:
  - All your ***achievements***—everything you've ever done in your life that you're pleased about

- Your **knowledge** and **skills**
- Your **best traits** and **attributes**

Once the three lists are complete, say to yourself: *I'm strong in many ways. I've learned a lot, and I've accomplished a lot in my life. With effort, I can do almost anything I really want to do.* Repeat this sentence three times.

Every time you feel unsure of yourself and you tackle the task anyway, you strengthen your self-confidence. Even if you don't have the know-how, you can acquire it as you go—millions of successful people have done this. Consciously acknowledge what you're learning from these experiences and discuss them with someone who will listen and encourage you.

"Whatever you can do or dream you can, begin it; boldness has genius, power, and magic in it."

Johann Wolfgang von Goethe, German poet

Believe you can reach your goal, and you'll be halfway there.

"Persons of high self-esteem are not driven to make themselves superior to others; their joy is being who they are, not in being better than someone else."

Nathaniel Branden, American psychotherapist

"He that respects himself is safe from others. He wears a coat of mail that none can pierce."

Henry Wadsworth Longfellow, American poet

"Friendship with oneself is all-important, because without it one cannot be friends with anyone else in the world."

Eleanor Roosevelt, American diplomat

"We must not allow other people's limited perceptions to define us."

Virginia Satir, American psychologist

5

Self-Esteem

Be your own best friend, and you'll be a better friend to others.

Whenever I think about positive self-esteem and its importance to personal achievement, mental health, and happiness, I think of how perilous a life journey can be. And I always think of Chuck.

Chuck was the second child in a large Catholic family. His parents were good people. His dad was a petty officer in the Navy, which meant he had to deploy on a regular basis and was absent from the family for months at a time. Chuck's mom loved nurturing small children, which is probably why she had so many of them. By necessity, she had to give most of her attention to the smaller ones. Still, it was the kind of family environment in which a child could grow up to live a productive life. And most of them did.

But not Chuck. I knew Chuck in high school. He and I were on the golf team together, and walking around the course, we had ample time to get to know each other. I was intrigued by him because he was a better golfer than I was. Still, he often cheated by surreptitiously replacing lost balls, improving the lie of his ball on the fairway, and entering inaccurate scores on his card.

He lied about a lot of other things, too, but I was able to piece together much of his life history. His older brother, Mark, who went to the same high school, was a straight-A student. He was the student body president and the valedictorian at graduation. He went to UCLA on a National Merit scholarship. I always thought Mark was a great guy, but Chuck expressed a kind of petty bitterness towards him. I knew that Chuck had grown up in the shadow of his high-achieving older brother, and so he never felt adequate. Mark was smarter, more athletic, better-looking, and more popular—seemingly superior in every way.

In my opinion, Chuck brought a lot of his problems on himself. While Mark was an Eagle Scout, Chuck started a forest fire playing with matches. He was caught shoplifting. He wrecked the family car. And the day before graduation, he slammed a hammer into one wall locker after another as he walked down the hall for the last time. It seemed to me that he was angry because he received a lot of criticism and censure, not the approval he craved. And, of course, his actions damaged his low self-esteem even more, creating a vicious cycle.

The year I entered West Point, Chuck enlisted in the Air Force. When I was a cadet, the plebes (first-year students) weren't allowed to go home for Christmas—a silly tradition that has since been corrected. But I remember how cheered I was to have a phone call from Chuck during the holidays. When I asked him what he was doing, he said he was on leave from duty in Vietnam. He said he had seen combat and had been awarded a Bronze Star. Much later, I found out that he was stationed in Korea—not Vietnam—and instead of a combat decoration, he received a Dishonorable Discharge from the Air Force because of alcoholism problems.

Years later I happened to see him during a visit to my hometown. He seemed hyperactive and overly talkative, bragging about things I no longer remember. It occurred to me that Chuck would lie about anything, even the weather. Ordinary life just wasn't good enough; he had to embellish everything. Then he asked me if I'd sponsor him on the PGA Tour. I kept my thoughts to myself, but when I told him that I wasn't financially able to help him out, he accused me of being a disloyal friend.

I never saw him again after that. I heard from his older brother that he had seduced the wife of his younger brother and was now an outcast in his own family. The last I heard, he was gunned down in front of a convenience store in Miami, presumably a drive-by revenge shooting. The case was never solved, and there was no funeral.

It's a tragic story, and at the bottom, it's about the importance of positive self-esteem.

According to psychotherapist and author Nathaniel Branden, author of *Six Pillars of Self-Esteem*, self-esteem is the belief that we are worthy of personal fulfillment and happiness. He makes the point that self-esteem isn't something that other people give you. You create your own self-esteem. Only you can decide how to think about yourself when life is difficult.

What is SELF-ESTEEM?

Self-esteem refers to your attitude about your own worth, including your feelings of self-acceptance and self-respect. Self-esteem is the foundation of your self-image and self-concept. To have healthy self-esteem, you need positive self-regard and a belief in your value as a person. Developing and maintaining a healthy level of self-esteem is an ongoing process that involves self-reflection, self-compassion, and cultivating a positive self-image based on realistic self-appraisal. The key is to give yourself credit for every good effort, every success, and every strength you have.

Why self-esteem is important:

Positive self-esteem is often associated with a greater sense of happiness, resilience, and overall well-being. Self-doubt can hold you back. Feelings of inadequacy can lead to fear of failure and a reluctance to assert yourself. And if you feel inadequate, you may be vulnerable to conformity and social pressure. You can be so sensitive to feedback or criticism that relationships and intimacy become difficult. Feelings of guilt and shame can lead to depression, neuroses, mental illness, and even suicide. In other words, if you don't feel you deserve happiness, you may do things that sabotage it.

"Nothing is a greater impediment to being on good terms with others than being ill at ease with yourself."

Honoré de Balzac, French novelist

What you can do to strengthen your self-esteem:

- ✓ Make a list of everything you've accomplished in your life.
- ✓ Nurture a realistic and positive view of who you are.
- ✓ Engage in positive self-talk. Make your inner dialogue supportive, encouraging, and compassionate. Focus on your strengths and acknowledge your achievements.
- ✓ Bounce back from setbacks by viewing them as learning opportunities rather than personal shortcomings.
- ✓ Express your needs, opinions, and boundaries assertively. Value your own perspective and rights while respecting those of others. Don't hesitate to speak up and assert your position in a respectful manner.
- ✓ Be a friend to yourself, practicing self-compassion and self-acceptance, embracing your imperfections, and treating yourself with kindness and understanding.
- ✓ When you finish an important task, celebrate.

- ✓ Think of a mistake you made or something you did that you regret. If you can, make amends. Then affirm what you learned from the experience and forgive yourself.

The more you nurture your self-esteem, the stronger it will become. It is always wise to partner with someone who will hold you accountable, guide you to learn from your efforts, and encourage you. This will help you stick with it and strengthen your self-esteem over time.

"Love yourself first and everything else falls into line. You really have to love yourself to get anything done in this world."

Lucille Ball, American comedian

Wear the armor of self-respect, and nothing will penetrate it.

"Humility is not thinking less of yourself but thinking of yourself less."

C.S. Lewis, British author

"There is no respect for others without humility in one's self."

Henri-Frederic Amiel, Swiss philosopher

"Pride divides the men, humility joins them."

Socrates, Greek philosopher

"It is unwise to be too sure of one's own wisdom. It is healthy to be reminded that the strongest might weaken and the wisest might err."

Mohandas Gandhi, Indian political leader

6

Humility

Everybody already knows you aren't perfect, so don't try to hide your imperfections.

Humility is the kind of strength that will help people see you as an honest, approachable, authentic individual. Without taking away from your strengths, you're willing to build on who you are by learning from others.

My favorite example of the power of humility is Mary Teresa Bojaxhiu, better known as Mother Teresa, who was an Albanian-Indian Catholic nun. She was born in 1910. At the age of 18, she left her home in Albania to join the Sisters of Loreto in Ireland. After training as a nurse, she arrived in India in 1929, and in 1960, she founded the Missionaries of Charity, which eventually expanded globally. The mission was simple yet profound: to provide "wholehearted and free service to the poorest of the poor."

Despite facing numerous challenges and limited resources, Mother Teresa spent her days in the slums of Kolkata, where she cared for the sick, fed the hungry, and comforted the dying. She lived a life of austerity, always putting the needs of others above her own.

While she received many awards for her humanitarian work, Mother Teresa never sought recognition or personal gain. In her acceptance speech for the Nobel Peace Prize in 1978, she spoke not of herself but of the desperate need to address poverty and suffering: "I accept the Nobel Prize in the name of the poor, the hungry, the naked, the homeless—of the crippled, the blind, the lepers, of all those people who feel unwanted, unloved, uncared for throughout society, people who have become a burden to the society and are shunned by everyone."

What is HUMILITY?

Humility means having a realistic, balanced view of who you are while honoring your kinship with the rest of humanity. Without seeking attention, you're comfortable acknowledging both your strengths and your limitations. It's about modesty—maintaining strong self-esteem and self-confidence without boasting or exaggerating your strengths and without giving in to egotism or self-centeredness.

Why humility is important:

It can be tempting to "toot your own horn," downplaying your shortcomings or exaggerating your accomplishments. By practicing genuine humility, people will see you as a balanced, honest, and authentic individual. They will come to believe that you aren't self-absorbed and that you care about them. Therefore, they'll respect you and trust you—even follow you.

"The first test of a truly great person is in their humility."

John Ruskin, British author

What you can do to strengthen your humility:

- ✓ Resist the temptation to boast or trumpet your accomplishments.

- ✓ Admit your mistakes. Don't try to shift blame onto others or make excuses for your actions.
- ✓ Instead of seeking personal recognition for success, share the credit, affirming what others have contributed.
- ✓ Appreciate that you have benefited from the assistance, support, or kindness of others. Express genuine gratitude for the people who have helped you along the way.
- ✓ Admit that you don't have all the answers and actively seek input from others.
- ✓ Be open to learning from anyone, regardless of their position or status. Listen with genuine interest and consider other viewpoints.
- ✓ Seek constructive feedback and express appreciation when you get it.
- ✓ When someone expresses appreciation, avoid false modesty. Simply thank them.

Humility is a behavior pattern. When you feel the urge to assert your considerable knowledge, skills, and experience, remember that there's a lot you don't know. Stay open to what you can learn from others. The more you exercise humility, the more you'll gain. To help you stick with it until humility is your established pattern, find someone who would be willing to discuss with you what you're learning, hold you accountable and offer encouragement.

"The higher we are placed, the more humbly we should walk."

Marcus Tullius Cicero

Stay teachable, regardless of what you already know.

"Opportunity dances with those who are already on the dance floor."

H. Jackson Brown, American author

"Let your hook always be cast. In the pool where you least expect it, will be a fish."

Ovid, Roman poet

"Life is not a matter of holding good cards, but sometimes playing a poor hand well."

Jack London, American novelist

"Out of clutter, find Simplicity. From discord, find Harmony. In the middle of difficulty lies Opportunity."

Albert Einstein, American physicist

7

Optimism

Look for the bright side—the other half of reality.

One of my best friends confided in me that, in the early stages of an important project, he worried a lot that it wouldn't work out.

"Were your fears justified?" I asked.

"I guess not. I've learned a lot since then and am a lot more confident now. Next time, I probably won't fret so much."

I told him, "Maybe instead of fretting, you could focus on the outcome you hope will happen."

There's a practical reason for doing this. When you worry, you imagine a negative outcome. You're afraid of the consequences if bad things *do* happen.

Some people say this is just being realistic, because bad things do happen.

I disagree. It's hard to do what you have to do to succeed if you've flooded your brain with images of failure. How can you make the best choices to create success when you aren't even thinking about a positive result? Why not choose to focus on the result you want instead? It's what you plan to work towards, after all. By thinking about where you want to go, you can make decisions about how to get there.

What is OPTIMISM?

Optimism is a hopeful, constructive attitude about life and the future. It's a mindset that, most of the time, you can deal with a challenge and create a positive result. When faced with setbacks, you look for the lessons and use them to fuel your growth and resilience. Optimism isn't a blind faith in positive outcomes or a guarantee of success. You don't ignore or deny problems. Instead, you achieve a balanced perspective, believing in your capacity to be proactive and do something about what's challenging you.

Why optimism is important:

Life and work can be unpredictable in a myriad of ways. You might make mistakes or fail to accomplish what you're trying to achieve. In order to deal with problems and overcome adversity, you need to believe in your ability to find solutions. While acknowledging the troubling downsides, to succeed you need to adopt an "eyes wide open" belief in the possibilities.

When the going gets tough, it's always a mixture of bad news and good news. Pessimism is when you focus strictly on the negative news. You fail to see the whole picture. It takes inner strength to also consider the positives because when the unexpected happens, it can take the wind out of your sails and create frustration, pain, and loss. At times like that, it's natural to focus on what's causing you distress. Instead, when you encounter adversity, be a *realist*.

The key to optimism is being realistic—the willingness to acknowledge the positives along with the negatives.

In other words, seek to understand both the negatives and the positives:

- Yes, your situation has disadvantages, but what are the *advantages?*

- You're faced with problems, but what *solutions* are possible?
- You're limited in what you can do, but what are the *opportunities?*
- There are constraints, but what *resources* are available to you?
- You may feel inadequate at the moment, but what do you have going for you—what are your *strengths?*
- Maybe certain people have let you down, but who are your *allies*—the people who want you to succeed?

"A wise man will make more opportunities than he finds."

Francis Bacon, British philosopher

What you can do to strengthen your optimism:

✓ The next time you face a challenge, setback, or failure, consider the positives as well as the negatives of your situation. Often you can learn from the experience and come out stronger in the end.

✓ If you are facing a tough financial time, commit to the possibility that, with creativity, hard work, and determination, you can improve your situation.

✓ Get in the habit of seeing the advantages as well as the disadvantages and solutions as well as problems. Focus on taking advantage of what you have rather than dwelling on what you lack.

✓ The next time you experience personal adversity, keep moving forward, staying focused on healing, growth, and achieving the best for your life.

- ✓ When starting something new, envision a successful outcome, even if there is uncertainty or risk involved.
- ✓ When hit with "the challenge of the week," make a list of the upsides, advantages, and possibilities in the situation.
- ✓ When faced with an everyday crisis, ask yourself: *What can I do to deal with this situation?*

As you work to become more optimistic, you can expect both successes and disappointments. Partner with someone to coach you and encourage you, then learn from your attempts, stick with it, and you'll get stronger over time.

"Every strike brings me closer to the next home run."

Babe Ruth, American professional baseball player

When the door of happiness slams shut, other doors will open for you.

"When the going gets tough, the tough get going."

Knute Rockne, American football coach

"Do not judge me by my success, judge me by how many times I fell down and got back up again."

Nelson Mandela, South African president

"You may have to fight a battle more than once to win it."

Margaret Thatcher, British prime minister

"It's not the strongest of a species that survive, nor the most intelligent, but the ones most resilient and responsive to change."

Charles Darwin, British scientist

8

Resilience

The next time you get knocked down, get back up.

In the fall of 1967, as a young second lieutenant, I found myself coming down the side of a north Georgia mountain in the Army Ranger School. It was tricky. I carried my M-16, a fifty-pound pack, and a radio on my back. I was being careful, but rocks beneath my feet suddenly came loose, and I landed on my back. My ranger buddy quickly came to my side to check me out. I felt a shooting pain in my left ankle. Was I injured? Would I be able to continue down the mountain? Several of my friends in the class had already left the training due to injury. The thought of having to be evacuated made me furious. I used my anger to stand up and completely dismissed the idea that I wouldn't be able to continue. I told my buddy, "I'm okay. I'm good."

And we continued down the mountain. I focused on doing what I had to do. Adrenaline was my friend. I didn't think of my ankle until we had established a camp for the night. Apparently, the injury wasn't serious enough to require medical attention, and I put the incident behind me.

Ranger School was fabulous training, for I would have to exercise resilience many times throughout my career. At the time, I didn't appreciate that one of the training objectives of Ranger

School was building this behavior pattern. The combat veterans who trained us knew what we'd be facing in the near future.

What is RESILIENCE?

Resilience is the ability to overcome the impact of a loss, failure, or disappointment—which can cause you to doubt your ability to continue striving:

- A negative performance evaluation
- Not being promoted or selected for an important assignment
- Serious illness or injury
- Inadvertently causing harm
- Criticism or disparagement from colleagues
- Bad feedback from customers
- Failure to win an important contract or sale
- Personal adversity, such as death in the family or relationship problems

Your ability to be resilient is made stronger as you work on several other character skills, such as self-awareness. perseverance, courage, composure, confidence, and optimism.

Why resilience is important:

Resilience is important for dealing with the many challenges of life. Setbacks are both common and unpredictable in the workplace, and it's important to recover quickly and continue to give your best effort. If you give up when the going gets tough, you lose the opportunity to succeed. You may even let down people who depend on you.

"We may encounter many defeats, but we must not be defeated."

Maya Angelou, American poet

What you can do to strengthen your resilience:

- ✓ Ask someone who cares about your success to be there to listen and encourage you when you need it.
- ✓ Start small. The next time you experience a minor disappointment, resolve to stick with it and come back stronger.
- ✓ When a situation causes you to doubt yourself, resolve to prepare better and tough it out.
- ✓ The next time you're faced with adversity, instead of complaining or making excuses, set aside feelings of disappointment and keep striving.
- ✓ After a mistake or failure, remember your strengths and proceed with confidence.
- ✓ "Look on the bright side" is not a silly saying. When a situation falls apart, accept reality and start looking for upsides, solutions, and opportunities.

Unexpected adversity is a part of life. Resilience is about coming back stronger and making this a behavior pattern. Like training a muscle, the more you exercise it, the stronger it will get. This process will be greatly aided by having a partner who will encourage you. If you learn from your attempts and stick with it, your resilience will build over time.

"What doesn't kill me, makes me stronger."

Friedrich Nietzsche, German philosopher

Don't quit. Go again. Endure. Prevail.

"Children need to be taught how to think, not what to think."

Margaret Mead, American anthropologist

"Think like a man of action, act like a man of thought."

Henri Bergson, French philosopher

"We can ignore reality, but we cannot ignore the consequences of ignoring reality."

Ayn Rand, American philosopher

"Reason can wrestle and overthrow terror."

Euripides, Greek playwright

9

Rationality

Pay attention to what reason teaches, or it will rap you on the knuckles.

From the newspaper: A man shot and killed his friend outside a bar. Apparently, the friend owed him money but refused to pay it. When their argument had gotten physical inside the bar, they were asked to leave. Out in the parking lot, one of the men pulled out a gun and fired twice at the other. The friend died at the scene.

Although violent and shocking, it is a familiar story—the kind of thing that happens in a big city. But I find it difficult to imagine the mindset of someone who would do that. One moment, the young man was angry; the next moment, his friend was dead, and he was in a police car headed toward a trial and a possible death sentence. His life was ruined.

What was he thinking? The answer is that he probably wasn't thinking much at all. He was reacting emotionally without letting the rational part of his mind help him decide what to do. And I thought: *Maybe being logical wasn't one of his strengths.*

We humans have advanced brains, but we aren't born to be rational. We have to learn how to think. When I was a young man, I wasn't as rational as I am now. People who know me might be surprised at that statement. I was never like the young man with the gun. Far from it. I was the top student in my class from the first grade all the way through high school. Even as a youth, I had good reasoning abilities.

But I also had the mind and heart of a poet. I wrote poetry in high school and was the editor of the literary magazine. I had a romantic, idealistic frame of mind. Later, at West Point, I published a few poems. My English professors were so impressed that after graduation, they arranged for me to get a degree in English at Duke University and return to West Point to teach. At Duke, my poems were published regularly in their literary journal, and one of them won the annual Academy of American Poets poetry prize. While teaching English at West Point, I co-authored a book of poems. It's who I was back then.

I recall an incident as a cadet in which I failed to think rationally. During my second year, I had a Sunday date with a charming young woman. As we walked along the Hudson River, I was so enthralled with her that I lost track of time and missed the required formation for supper. I had plenty of time to think about that during the coming month, when I reported for afternoon punishment marching sessions during the weekends, instead of spending more time with my lady friend.

West Point and my subsequent 20-year career in the Army were good for me this way. My duties required me to exercise logic so often that the pattern became a strength. I feel that today, my right brain and my left brain sing from the same sheet of music. I'm as reasonable, analytical, and strategic as I ever hope to be, and while I'm even more passionate and creative than ever, I exercise these strengths mostly to help others.

Life engages our emotions in almost everything we do. So, it's not always easy to be rational. But exercising that skill can help you get what you want. It can even save your life.

What is RATIONALITY?

Unlike other animals, humans can think before they react. Rationality is the use of critical thinking skills, which involve the objective evaluation of arguments, evidence, and information. Using logic, you can define a problem realistically, consider available options, assess potential risks and benefits, and select the most appropriate course of action. If you practice thinking things through, your ability to reason and act rationally will get stronger. You're likely to avoid mistakes that could result from acting impulsively without considering the consequences of your actions.

Why rationality is important:

Rationality helps you transcend personal biases and what you hope to be true. It's key to evaluating information, weighing evidence, and drawing practical, valid conclusions. With this kind of logical reasoning, you can assess the effectiveness of creative ideas, make sound decisions, and establish realistic plans.

How does one become more rational? According to Aristotle, one becomes more rational by thinking rational thoughts. Yes, you could learn to play chess, read more, and work crossword and Sudoku puzzles. But I think the best learning opportunities have to do with decisions. Think about the consequences of various courses of action. What are the risks? What are the rewards? What are the costs? What are the benefits? Spontaneity is fine, but if you can make yourself think things through, your ability to reason and act rationally will get stronger.

"It isn't enough to have a good mind; the main thing is to use it well."

Rene Descartes, French mathematician

What you can do to strengthen your rationality:

- ✓ Consider using the scientific method, which employs experimentation, gathering and observing the evidence, analyzing data objectively, and drawing conclusions based on this process.
- ✓ When interacting with people, try to assess accurately what they are thinking and feeling.
- ✓ When troubleshooting a problem or trying to fix something, use reasoning to pinpoint the actual cause.
- ✓ The next time you're faced with a tough decision, evaluate your options logically.
- ✓ When considering your options, assess the upsides and downsides.
- ✓ Before acting on a decision, ask whether it makes sense.
- ✓ When resolving conflict, consider objectively the perspectives and needs of others while engaging in constructive dialogue.
- ✓ Fight the tendency to take things for granted. Reach for a clear, detailed awareness of what's going on.
- ✓ When someone voices an opinion, whether you share their belief or not, do some checking to find out what the opinion is based on.
- ✓ Consider something you believe to be true. List the reasons why you believe that.

As you work to engage your rationality more often, you can expect both successes and disappointments. Partner with someone to coach you with encouragement, then learn from your attempts, stick with it, and you'll get stronger over time.

"Thought is great and swift and free, the light of the world, and the chief glory of man."

Bertrand Russell, British philosopher

Use common sense to an uncommon degree, and people will think you are wise.

"Take calculated risks. That is quite different from being rash."

George S. Patton, American general

"Courage is the first of the virtues, because it makes all others possible."

Aristotle, Greek philosopher

"A ship in port is safe, but that's not what ships are built for."

Grace Hopper, American admiral

"Let us be brave in the face of adversity."

Lucius Annaeus Seneca, Roman playwright

10

Courage

Leap the great leap, and you'll cross the chasm.

In 1980, I researched Army training practices to write a manual for junior leaders on how to train soldiers. I traveled to various units to observe best practices. One of these was Special Forces training at the John F. Kennedy Special Warfare Center at Fort Bragg, NC.

On the day I visited, trainees were being introduced to rappelling skills. About a dozen drill sergeants barked at the soldiers as they climbed the tower, learned how to tie a seat, and took their first descent over the edge. It was loud, chaotic, and stressful.

I decided I needed a closer look, so I climbed the tower myself. At the top, I witnessed young men struggling to maintain their composure under the pressure to perform and the fear of going over the side unassisted. I wondered if the stress created by the drill sergeants had a positive learning effect. I was jolted out of my musings by one of the sergeants who came up to me and said, "Well, Major, are you going to stand there and watch, or are you going over the side?"

With a challenge like that, how could I beg off?

What he didn't know was that I had mastered rappelling skills in the Army Ranger School. I had climbed 100-foot rock faces without safety ropes. I had rappelled down mountain cliffs numerous times.

So I quickly walked over, tied my seat, and went over the side. I negotiated the 30-foot distance in one leap, braking for a soft landing. I went to the bleachers and sat next to an old sergeant-major as I watched the trainees cope with their fear.

Soon, the session was over, and the sergeant-major invited me to stick around and watch the families of the cadre use the rappelling tower. This time, there was no shouting, only laughter and encouragement. It was just a bunch of women and kids having fun. I watched little ten-year-old girls playfully do what 20-year-old male Special Forces trainees struggled to do. The kids saw the rappelling tower as some super-cool jungle gym. They had no fear at all, so the rappelling activity was ridiculously easy. They climbed the tower over and over. They couldn't get enough of it.

What I learned from this is that fear arises from our perception of the situation, which can vary from person to person. The rappel was exactly the same challenge for both the soldiers and the kids, but the soldiers had to face their fears in order to do it. They risked failure, humiliation, disqualification, and, they thought, personal injury. For those who succeeded—and not all of them did—it was a big deal. The training gave them a victory of courage and self-confidence.

The soldiers who successfully completed the many months of Special Forces training would later survive more challenges to their courage. In the end, they would become experts in dealing with fear—icons of mental toughness, ready for anything.

I've faced some interesting dangers in my life. In Vietnam, I was an advisor to Vietnamese infantry soldiers. This meant that I was involved in some kind of combat operation several times a week—airmobile assaults, search-and-destroy missions, night ambushes, and so forth.

I came under fire more times than I can remember, but I don't remember being afraid. For me, the main feeling was irritation. I was angry that someone was trying to kill us and that I would now have to deal with it.

Mostly, I remember concentrating on managing all the activities related to close combat. I had to have a clear head to keep higher headquarters informed, assess the situation, communicate with my Vietnamese counterpart, direct movement and fire, deal with problems, request fire support or medical evacuation, and manage it when it arrived. Naturally, a person couldn't do all that if he felt fear. If fear raised its ugly head, it had to be shoved aside. Lives depended on it.

I remember being afraid one night in 2001. The economy had been in a recession after the stock market "tech bubble" burst. When it looked like the economy might recover, 9/11 happened, which caused confidence in the economy to tank even further. My business was to supply organizations with learning and development resources, and funds for tools like these were the first to be cut off. Our sales plummeted, with no hope in sight. I remember thinking that something dramatic was about to happen to my company. We might even go out of business. I imagined the scenarios, and yes, I felt real fear. But we focused on creative solutions, and wonderful things have happened for us since then.

Fear is a healthy, natural emotion. It's a whole-body alarm to help you sense danger so you can do what you need to do to avoid loss, harm, or death. A lot of threatening things can happen in a normal life. The question is, when it happens, what will you do next? Will you act to prevent loss, harm, or death? Will you take a chance to open a door of opportunity?

I find Norman Vincent Peale's words comforting: "Too much caution is bad for you. By avoiding things you fear, you may let yourself in for unhappy consequences. It is usually wiser to stand up to a scary-seeming experience and walk right into it, risking the bruises and hard knocks. You are likely to find it is not as tough as you had thought. Or you may find it plenty tough, but also discover you have what it takes to handle it."

What is COURAGE?

When you feel discomfort or fear in an unknown or dangerous situation, courage is about thinking before you react. When faced with a worrisome situation, it's natural to feel anxiety or fear—your body's instinctive response. By setting aside your instinctive reaction long enough to think before you act, you can evaluate your situation—the risks and rewards—to decide what you should do and take effective action.

Why courage is important:

While fear is a natural and useful reaction to danger, if it continues to dominate your response, you probably won't be able to do what needs to be done. Instead of retreating to safety, success will come from setting fear aside so you can evaluate the situation, take prudent risks, and deal with it.

"Without courage, wisdom bears no fruit."

Baltasar Gracian, Spanish prince

What you can do to strengthen your courage:

- ✓ When faced with discrimination, oppression, or wrongdoing, take a stand for your principles by advocating for your rights and the rights of others.
- ✓ Express and defend your beliefs in spite of opposition. Voice an unpopular opinion, advocate for a cause, and refuse to compromise your values.
- ✓ Resist peer pressure to stay true to your personal values and principles.

- ✓ Take calculated risks while starting a new business, pursuing a challenging career change, or embarking on an adventure outside your comfort zone.
- ✓ Persist to overcome a personal fear or anxiety, such as a phobia.
- ✓ Exercise courage when engaging in extreme sports or activities that require overcoming physical limitations.
- ✓ Take bold action at work or in your life.
- ✓ Speak your mind regardless of how it may be received.
- ✓ When you notice people you know doing things that you don't approve of, stand your ground. Don't follow the herd.

The idea in all these actions is to keep fear from becoming a paralyzing emotion. If you feel fear, pay attention to it, but then quickly put it aside long enough to assess the nature of the risk. What are the chances that bad things could happen? How bad? What are your choices? What are the risks and the benefits of these options? I recommend that you work with a coach to discuss your experiences and learn from them.

"Take a chance! All life is a chance. The man who goes farthest is generally the one who is willing to do and dare."

Dale Carnegie, American author

Confront the unknown, and its face will become familiar to you.

"Tough times never last, but tough people do."

Robert Schuller, American clergyman

"If you are patient in a single moment of anger, you will avoid a hundred moments of sorrow."

Chinese Proverb

"Anyone can steer a ship when the sea is calm."

Harvey Mackay, American author

"If you can't stand the heat, get out of the kitchen."

Harry Truman, American president

11

Composure

When emotions blow, bend like grass. In the quiet, you'll stand tall.

It has been over 50 years since my years as a cadet at West Point, and I'm sure the institution has made many changes since then. However, back then, in addition to being physically and academically challenging, plebe (freshman) year was a period of trial and indoctrination. During that first year, I experienced countless stressful encounters with upperclassmen. For example, during meals, I had to sit on the front edge of my chair at rigid attention. At any moment during the meal, an upperclassman at my table might shout, "Mr. Coates, what's for supper, and what's the movie tonight?"

Plebes were required to memorize and recite these details on command.

"Sir, for supper, we are having baked ham, snowflake potatoes, and mixed vegetables. For dessert, we have carrot cake. The movie for tonight is "From Russia with Love," starring Sean Connery."

"A James Bond flick, huh?"

"Yes, sir."

"Who's the female star?"

I didn't reply right away. Sweat broke out on my forehead and upper lip as I frantically searched my memory. If I wanted to eat my lunch, I had to have the answer.

"Well?" the upperclassman demanded.

I gave my memory one last search. Nothing. "Sir, I do not know."

The upperclassman slammed his fist on the table and shifted his attention to my classmate seated next to me.

"Mr. Kovak, who's the female lead?"

"Sir, the female lead of tonight's move is..." I hated that my classmate was put on the spot because I had failed to remember what I was required to know.

"Daniela Bianchi," he said. *He knew!*

"Right! Good work, Kovak! Fall out. Relax and enjoy your lunch. Not you, Coates. How come you didn't know that?"

"No excuse, sir."

"Bang your head in, mister! Don't you know that the female lead is the most important fact about a movie? Bang your head in!" he shouted with genuine outrage. "Now, give me The Days."

At the end of that ordeal, he said, "Listen, Coates, you're supposed to know this stuff cold. I want you to come around to my room tonight at nineteen hundred hours. Full dress gray and be ready for inspection. And I'll want to hear The Days again. If you know what's good for you, you'll get it right this time, Smackhead."

Talk about stress! Actually, incidents like these were a frequent fact of life during my freshman year. I hated it. But it taught me to keep my cool. To survive, I had to learn to face this kind of pressure calmly so I could do what I had to do. None of my classmates who failed to learn composure survived Plebe Year. Which was the whole point. In combat, bad things happen, and you have to do hard things anyway, no matter what. Human lives are at stake.

And in the end, all this dealing with pressure served me well. During my years as a lieutenant in the Army, I faced much more intense situations—Ranger School, early command of a Hawk missile battery in Germany, and a combat tour as an infantry advisor in Vietnam. By the time I experienced my first firefight, I had become a kind of ninja grandmaster in the composure department. To this day, nothing rattles me.

Not everyone receives this kind of military training or gets the chance to serve in combat. Not everyone has to save a life, fight a fire, or enforce the law. Not everyone has to face danger on a regular basis.

But sooner or later, something will happen to you that will upset you. At some point, you'll be faced with an unexpected problem, disappointment, frustration, risk, or loss. As they say, "Stuff happens." Somebody will let you down. Someone won't do what you were expecting them to do. They might even work against you. Too many problems all at once can push you to your limit. And when this happens, your emotions will surge and begin to cloud your mind and impair your judgment.

The all-important question is, what will you do then? Will you panic? Will you lose your temper? Will you lash out in anger? Will the logical part of your brain stop working?

Or will you keep a cool head? Will you be mentally tough?

When you feel your emotions rising, mentally take a step back. Refuse to say or do anything for a moment. If you don't focus on and feed your emotions, they'll subside. Then you can more calmly think about your situation. You can do what has to be done and say what has to be said so people don't get hurt, damage is minimized, and problems get solved.

What is COMPOSURE?

Composure is the opposite of panic. It means keeping a cool head in a crisis—maintaining a calm demeanor in the face of adversity. This doesn't mean shutting down your emotions; it means being aware of your emotions and focusing instead on effective action. You respond appropriately rather than reacting impulsively.

Why composure is important:

Faced with an emergency or a critical, high-stress situation, you need to stay poised so you can think clearly and make rational decisions. When the stakes are high, or a situation is dangerous or life-threatening, it's natural for strong emotions to kick in. To deal with this kind of adversity, you need to set these emotions aside.

"Good judgment, common sense, and reason all fly out the window when emotions kick down your door."

John Wooden, American college basketball coach

What you can do to strengthen your composure:

- ✓ The next time you're faced with an emergency, stay calm and focused so you can make sound decisions, communicate effectively, and provide leadership.
- ✓ When faced with conflicts or disagreements, listen attentively, express yourself clearly and respectfully, and explore solutions without escalating tensions.
- ✓ When responding to criticism or negative feedback, stay calm and open-minded. Listen to understand, reflect on the feedback, and acknowledge it without reacting defensively or emotionally.
- ✓ When facing personal setbacks, such as a failure or disappointment, ask yourself: *What can I do now to make the best of this situation?*
- ✓ When driving during rush hour, tell yourself to stay calm, go with the flow, and drive safely.

- ✓ When someone is upset with you, instead of letting their comments trigger a negative reaction, consider that no one is perfect and they're just expressing their frustration.
- ✓ To stay calm during an interview, project an image of professionalism and confidence while answering questions, even if you feel nervous.
- ✓ When delivering a speech or presentation to a large audience, to control nervousness, maintain a steady voice, and project confidence.

As you work on improving your ability to stay composed in adverse situations, you can expect both successes and disappointments. Partner with someone to coach you with encouragement, then learn from your attempts, stick with it, and you'll get stronger over time.

"He that composes himself is wiser than he that composes books."

Benjamin Franklin, American scientist

If you fly into a rage, expect bruises when you crash.

"It is a great thing to know the season for speech and the season for silence."

Lucius Annaeus Seneca, Roman playwright

"Some things arrive on their own mysterious hour, on their own terms and not yours, to be seized or relinquished forever."

Gail Godwin, American novelist

"No great thing is created suddenly."

Epictetus, Greek philosopher

"All men commend patience, although few are willing to practice it."

Thomas ã Kempis, German author

12

Patience

Know when now isn't the right time, and you'll be ready when it is.

After a visit with friends in Nashville, torrential rains and street flooding kept us from the airport, so we returned to San Antonio a day late. And our plane was a half-hour behind schedule. I was tired and eager to get home. I could feel my patience wearing thin.

When we arrived at our car, we were surprised to find that the battery was dead. My wife suggested that airport security might be able to give us a jump. As we walked back to the terminal, I felt distressed and unhappy. We should have been on our way home by now. It was frustrating to have to deal with this. Why was the battery dead? Would we be able to find a security officer? Would he be able to help us? I recognized that this was one of those situations where I'd have to make an effort to stay calm and be patient. I've been in a gazillion situations like this.

Haven't you?

Thirty years ago, I lived near Yorktown, Virginia, and worked at the Armed Forces Staff College in Norfolk, nearly fifty miles away. It was a long commute and included the Hampton Roads Bridge Tunnel, which was famous for stop-and-go traffic, especially in the summer. On a good day, when traffic was flowing nicely, I could make the trip in about an hour, door-to-door.

I clearly remember a time when I wanted to get home "on time" because we had dinner reservations. On the bridge leading to the tunnel, traffic slowed to a stop. A half-mile ahead at the tunnel entrance, cars were motionless. I remember shouting several of my favorite obscenities and pounding on the steering wheel. They didn't have cell phones back then.

I'm not sure how or why, but days later, I got the brilliant idea of keeping books and audio cassettes in the car—something to do when traffic stopped. The idea was to make good use of the time. And it worked. When I got stuck on I-64, I reached for a book I was reading. Time flew by, the traffic started up again, and I learned some things. Cool.

I also learned this valuable lesson: *When you have to wait, you're in control of how you use the time.* You can spend it fuming, with all the well-known harmful side effects. Or you can spend it thinking about something interesting. Or you can get into the moment—enjoy the afternoon cast of light on the water, the gulls playing in the ocean breeze overhead. Or you can listen to an audio or read a book—get smarter by the minute. You're in charge. Spend the time any way you want. It doesn't have to be time wasted or time lost.

Patience has never come easy for me. I'm usually working on things I feel are important, and it usually takes three times as long as I foresaw to get things done. If I wanted to, I could make myself—and the people around me—miserable by being impatient. I've had feedback about this, and I've tried to get stronger in this area.

Several months ago, I was on my way to the grocery store when I got stuck behind a car going 30 mph in a 45 mph zone. I looked in the rear-view mirror, and the car behind me was uncomfortably close. I could have honked or flashed my lights, or I could have tried passing, but there was a lot of traffic, and it seemed unsafe. The store was only three miles away, so I just followed along.

Going down a row in the store parking lot, I saw that the car ahead of me had stopped completely. I waited for him to move, but I quickly realized that instead of finding a spot in a less crowded area, he was waiting for someone to return to his car. I had no idea how long he would do this. I could have risked backing up against the flow of traffic, or I could have honked my horn. I waited four or five minutes until a spot opened up for him, and I was able to pass.

Inside the store, I wheeled my cart along the dairy aisle. An elderly woman was standing next to her cart in the middle of the aisle, making it impossible to pass. I stopped my cart short of hers, but she didn't seem to notice me. I waited a minute while she gazed up at the shelves. She appeared bewildered at all the choices. I said in my gentlest voice, "Excuse me. May I pass?" She seemed surprised. I smiled and thanked her as she maneuvered her cart to one side.

On my list was "candied ginger." I don't know what candied ginger is, and I wouldn't recognize it if I saw it. But I knew that if I could find some and bring it home, my wife would use it to make something wonderful. I asked the first employee I saw, a young man: "Can you tell me where to find candied ginger?" We made the tour of the store. "Well, it should be over here..." Finally, I suggested that if he didn't know where it was, perhaps someone else might know. So he found his supervisor, who took me right to it. Maybe the young man should have done that in the first place, but he seemed new and was eager to please.

At the cash register, a customer seemed to be having trouble paying. Maybe it was an equipment malfunction, or maybe his card wasn't reading properly. I couldn't tell. The lady in front of me rolled her eyes and turned away with a sour look. This trip to the store was taking a lot longer than I thought it would.

Standing by my cart, I began thinking about my outline for some content I was writing.

By the time I left the store with my purchases, it was pouring down rain. Great. I didn't know rain was in the forecast, so I hadn't brought an umbrella. I looked at the sky and hoped it was a passing shower. I was right. In a few minutes, only light rain fell, and I walked to my car.

Patience served me well quite a few times that day.

What is PATIENCE?

Sometimes, there are factors beyond your control. Patience involves waiting calmly until the most effective time to act. This could mean enduring adversity, delay, or provocation without becoming frustrated or agitated. When you have an urgent need or are in a hurry, you do what you can, but you accept that some things can't be rushed. You control your emotions when things aren't going your way. It helps to have a tolerant and understanding attitude towards obstacles or the behavior of others.

Why patience is important:

You need patience because as you try to achieve a goal, it's likely the unexpected will happen. Patience will improve your decision-making because it will help you calmly assess whether you can realistically do something about a situation. Recognizing that a situation is one you can't control prevents you from acting inappropriately. With patience, you can handle setbacks, difficulties, or inconveniences without becoming overly stressed or reacting impulsively.

"Make the best use of what is in your power, and take the rest as it happens."

Epictetus, Greek philosopher

What you can do to strengthen your patience:

- ✓ When waiting in a long line, whether at a grocery store or any crowded place, instead of getting upset, observe the people around you or spend time thinking about something that interests you.
- ✓ While teaching people a new skill, especially if they are novices and struggling, instead of becoming irritated, help them learn at their own pace.
- ✓ When dealing with technical difficulties, such as a slow internet connection or a problem with an electronic device, rather than getting frustrated, focus on methodically troubleshooting the issue.
- ✓ When dealing with a conflict, take the time to listen to the other person's perspective to understand their needs and concerns.
- ✓ When working towards a long-term goal, keep in mind that unforeseen setbacks are common.
- ✓ When recovering from an injury or illness, follow your treatment plan, engage in rehabilitation, and give your body time to heal.
- ✓ While nurturing a new relationship, invest time and effort to build a meaningful connection.
- ✓ When learning a difficult skill, acknowledge that progress is probably going to be slow at first but that with consistent practice, gradual improvement is possible.
- ✓ When in slow traffic, focus on safety and remind yourself that it's okay if you arrive late.
- ✓ When someone you're talking to is having a hard time getting to the point, use your best listening skills.

You don't have to seek opportunities to practice patience; they happen often enough. Do your best to take advantage of them to reinforce the behavior pattern of patience until it becomes your automatic response to frustrating situations. There will be times when you forget, and you become impatient. You can learn from these experiences, too. In other words, be patient with yourself! And it really helps to have someone willing to listen to your accounts of successes and failures and give you encouragement to stick with it.

"There is a time to let things happen and a time to make things happen."

Hugh Prather, American author

Be willing to wait, and things that can't be hurried will happen anyway.

PART TWO

BUILDING STRONGER RELATIONSHIPS

We need to be strong for what life will require of us, and that includes being strong to nurture our relationships. We have a deeply ingrained need for human relationships, and very little gets done in life without working well with others. But every person is unique, and establishing mutually rewarding relationships takes work. In this section, I describe 12 character skills that are particularly important for managing relationships:

13. Honesty
14. Integrity
15. Appreciation
16. Forgiveness
17. Empathy
18. Compassion
19. Generosity
20. Fairness
21. Loyalty
22. Trust
23. Cooperation
24. Service

"Every violation of truth is not only a sort of suicide in the liar, but is a stab at the health of human society."

Ralph Waldo Emerson, American philosopher

"To be completely honest with oneself is the very best effort a human being can make."

Sigmund Freud, Austrian psychoanalyst

"A liar will not be believed, even when he speaks the truth."

Aesop, Greek storyteller

"The truth is more important than the facts."

Frank Lloyd Wright, American architect

13

Honesty

Make truth your foundation, and the edifice you build on it will last.

My wife sometimes tells me stories about her time as a young commercial banker in Houston in the 1980s. Oil prices had fallen drastically, so her client portfolio consisted mostly of "work-out projects"—finding ways to help businesses repay loans before they defaulted. It was a stressful time.

She worked for a small community bank run by the founder. When she took over the portfolio, she reviewed the loans and discovered one that should never have been made in the first place. Her recommendation was to downgrade the loan, require additional sources of repayment, and establish a timetable for repayment. She gave the chairman a list of actions needed to qualify the loan for renewal.

When he told her to renew it as it was, she stood her ground. Otherwise, she'd have to tell the committee that the loan was acceptable as it stood, which wasn't true.

The chairman was upset and renewed the loan anyway. Several months later, a team of bank examiners questioned her about the loan. They told her the chairman said she was the one who approved it. She was outraged and produced her copy of the list of requirements she had given to him.

A few weeks later, he was fired.

Back then, my wife was single, and she dated an attractive, intelligent young man who shared many of her interests, such as photography and running. The relationship looked promising.

One day, he was showing her a stack of recent photos he'd taken. At the bottom of the stack was a picture of a woman's hands holding an engagement ring.

She asked about the ring and the woman holding it. Looking at the floor, he said, "It's my fiancé."

Shocked, she replied, "But you said you weren't married."

"I'm not."

"Are you going to marry her?"

"Yes, someday."

My wife realized that she had been told a half-truth, which is just as insidious as a lie. "Why didn't you tell me you were engaged?"

He mumbled his excuses, and she realized he had a serious character flaw and couldn't be trusted. The relationship was over.

And so it goes.

Every time you open your mouth, you have an opportunity to either provide true, accurate information or misrepresent the truth in some way. You could leave out an embarrassing fact, make the truth seem better than it really is, or say things that aren't true in hopes that the fabrication will give you a better chance of getting what you want.

But...

My wife once asked me, "Wasn't that the best coconut cake you ever had in your life?"

Well now. Was it? Actually, I had eaten a piece of coconut cake a few months earlier, and it was pretty awesome. Was this better? Maybe it was. Maybe it wasn't. But I knew what I should say.

"This is quite definitely the best coconut cake I've ever had," I said.

You see, my wife wasn't asking for the truth. She was asking for praise. She had worked hard to make this cake special, so I told her what she wanted to hear. And my spirit was right. I *loved* the cake. It was wonderful.

Every individual has to make these judgments. Yes, it can be tricky. But knowing what to say is actually not that hard. Do people need and expect the truth from you? If so, give it to them.

Every time.

What is HONESTY?

Honesty means being truthful, sincere, frank, and candid in your words. It means being transparent and genuine. You present information, thoughts, and feelings accurately and without deception, even when the truth is embarrassing, unpopular, or prevents you from enjoying a desired benefit. Honesty is the opposite of lying or any form of misleading communication.

Why honesty is important:

Dishonesty does damage. And you are the first to be damaged. You lose self-esteem every time you tell a lie. It's automatic. You know you lied. You know you're a person who tells lies. The people you lie to will be hurt if they make commitments based on the false information.

If you tell a lie, you have to maintain it. You have to keep track of what you said and tell follow-up lies to support your story. You have to remember those lies, too, which is terribly difficult. This is why lies are discovered most of the time. People eventually learn the truth.

All relationships are based on trust. Honesty is crucial to strong leadership, teamwork, or any meaningful relationship. People learn to trust you when they believe what you say is true. Without the trust of the people around you, you have nothing.

When they find out you've deceived them, they'll stop trusting you. They'll believe that if you lied once, you'll probably do it again. And they're right. It could take years to earn someone's trust, but you'll lose it in a single moment of betrayal. If people can't trust you to be honest, they won't trust you to act in their best interests, which could lead them to withdraw cooperation and engagement.

"A half-truth is a whole lie."

Jewish Proverb

What you can do to strengthen your honesty:

- ✓ When someone asks you a question, give an accurate answer, even if it makes you feel uncomfortable.
- ✓ When you've made a mistake or acted inappropriately, admit it and take responsibility.
- ✓ When you share your thoughts, feelings, or concerns, be open and sincere.
- ✓ Be honest with yourself. Admit the truth about your strengths, weaknesses, thoughts, feelings, desires, and motivations.
- ✓ When you say or do something you'd like to take back, tell the truth about your mistake.
- ✓ Recognize that no one expects you to be perfect and that most people appreciate candor. Admit your error without worrying about being embarrassed.

Like any skill, honesty is a behavior pattern. Choose honesty consistently, and it will get stronger over time. Partner with someone you trust to be honest with you and coach you with encouragement so you stick with it.

"When in doubt, tell the truth."

Mark Twain, American novelist

Say what you mean, and people will take you seriously.

"The truth of the matter is that you always know the right thing to do. The hard part is doing it."

H. Norman Schwarzkopf, American general

"He who accepts evil without protesting against it is really cooperating with it."

Henry David Thoreau, American philosopher

"A reputation for good judgment, for fair dealing, for truth, and for rectitude, is itself a fortune."

Henry Ward Beecher, American author

"I would prefer even to fail with honor than win by cheating."

Sophocles, Greek playwright

14

Integrity

Make sure your video matches your audio, and your show will get rave reviews.

When I was a West Point cadet, integrity was embodied in the Cadet Honor Code, which stated, "A cadet will not lie, cheat or steal or tolerate those who do." Honor violations were reported by fellow cadets and thoroughly investigated. Cadets found guilty were dismissed immediately. I had a friend who got married while he was a cadet, a fact which he kept secret. The problem was that he signed a statement every time he returned from leave declaring that he wasn't married. Eventually, this lie bothered him so much that he turned himself in the day before graduation. It was an honorable thing to do, but he was not allowed to graduate or to be commissioned as a second lieutenant.

I'll start by putting my working definition on the table: Integrity is doing what you've led others to believe you'll do.

Wherever a lot of power or money is involved, you're likely to find violations of integrity. Financiers, CEOs, and politicians are especially vulnerable. A politician who doesn't walk his talk? Uh-huh. The opportunity to do the wrong thing for personal gain can be so tempting that people lie, cheat, or steal to get ahead. Unfortunately, we live in a world where violations of integrity often go unpunished.

In 2009, the poster-monster for a lack of integrity had to be Bernie Madoff. For over 20 years, he misled thousands of wealthy investors by using a massive Ponzi scheme to defraud them of over $60 billion. This set some kind of world record for "breaking trust." His deception was not only a colossal example of a lack of integrity, it was also a felony—several felonies. He was convicted and sentenced to 150 years in prison. While imprisoned, he was admitted to the Duke Medical Center for "serious facial injuries."

From the likes of Madoff to simply being late to meetings, failures of integrity take many forms. But integrity is integrity, and when people don't honor their commitments, the first consequence is a loss of trust. People discover they can't count on someone to do what they need them to do. If someone is in a position of authority involving trust, the next consequence should be removal from that position.

I once had a friend who had some information I needed to complete a database. I asked him if he'd send me a file, and he said he'd be glad to. But he didn't. A week later, I contacted him, and he said he'd been busy, but he'd send it to me right away. He never did. And I never found out why because I never asked. I concluded I couldn't trust him to take care of a simple promise. I got the information I needed from someone else.

I think of integrity as a character skill because doing the right thing often means doing the hard thing. It may be inconvenient or difficult to keep your word. Or you may be tempted to do something else.

Here's food for thought: What would you do if no one was looking? Would you do the right thing even if you knew for sure that no one would ever know the difference? Say you're at a convenience store, and you buy a lottery ticket for a dollar. You hand the clerk a $10 bill. Distracted by her conversation with the other clerk, she puts your money in the register, gives you the ticket, and then counts out $19 in change. Clearly, the honorable thing is to point out her error and get the correct change. But many people would rationalize that no one was harmed and that it's a bit of luck that balances out all those past lottery losses.

Integrity hangs in the balance.

"Honesty" and "integrity" are common terms, but I often see them being used interchangeably. Sure, they're closely related, but to me, they're two different things. Honesty has to do with *communicating* the truth—what you say. Integrity has to do with *living* the truth—what you *do*.

So, I believe it's important to define "integrity." The more clearly you understand it, the more likely you'll be to act honorably and the less tolerant you'll be of people who act dishonorably.

What is INTEGRITY?

While honesty is spoken truth, integrity is truth in action. It means "walking your talk." By expressing your values and principles with your behavior, you demonstrate that you're the kind of person you've led people to believe you are. People know that it's not always easy to do the right thing; they will respect you for demonstrating integrity. They'll learn that you're reliable and trustworthy because you fulfill your promises and consistently do what is right.

This definition applies whether you sign a written contract, make a verbal promise, or present yourself to others as someone who lives according to your core values or a recognized code of ethics. It applies whether your actions are consciously planned or triggered by impulse or emotion.

Why integrity is important:

Being true to yourself is as important as being true to others. For example, if you resolve to quit snacking between meals, and then you reach for the peanuts and beer anyway, you're breaking a promise you made to yourself. The consequence? Subconsciously, you'll see yourself as someone who has trouble following through on commitments. Any loss of self-esteem is critical; it can hold you back from achievement and success.

Integrity is vital to leadership and teamwork. It's key to building strong relationships, which are based on trust. You create a positive reputation and a sense of reliability. People will trust that you'll "watch their back," meaning that as they face challenges, you'll support them and help them be successful.

"When you say you'll do it, do it. Don't give your word unless you intend to keep it."

John Wooden, American college basketball coach

What you can do to strengthen your integrity:

- ✓ Always ask yourself: *Is this the right thing to do?*
- ✓ When tempted to do something you might regret, imagine the possible consequences.
- ✓ Do your best to follow through on your promises, whether they are personal, professional, or social.
- ✓ Do everything you can to meet deadlines and honor agreements.
- ✓ Always maintain the privacy of information shared in confidence, whether it's personal or professional.
- ✓ Before you make a choice, ask yourself if it aligns with your moral compass and ethical principles, even when you're faced with difficult or tempting circumstances.
- ✓ Treat others with dignity, empathy, and fairness.
- ✓ Stand up against dishonesty, corruption, or unethical practices, even if it means going against the norm or facing potential repercussions.

- ✓ When you find a lost item, try to locate its rightful owner and return it.
- ✓ Consider whether what you're about to do will cause people to respect and trust you.

For integrity to become a behavior pattern, you need to exercise it consistently over time. To stay committed, ask someone to talk with you frequently to discuss your experiences, encourage you, and hold you accountable.

"Happiness is when what you think, what you say, and what you do are in harmony."

Mohandas Gandhi, Indian political leader

Close the door on lesser evils, and you'll shut out the greater ones as well.

"Oppression involves a failure of the imagination: the failure to imagine the full humanity of other human beings."

Margaret Atwood, Canadian novelist

"Diversity makes for a rich tapestry, and we must understand that all the threads of the tapestry are equal in value no matter what their color."

Maya Angelou, American author

"Appreciation is a wonderful thing: It makes what is excellent in others belong to us as well."

Voltaire, French Enlightenment writer

"We need to give each other the space to grow, to be ourselves, to exercise our diversity. We need to give each other space so that we may both give and receive such beautiful things as ideas, openness, dignity, joy, healing, and inclusion."

Max De Pree, American businessman and writer

15

Appreciation

Look for the best in people, and you'll have cause to celebrate.

My wife once asked me: "I got an email from a gardening blog buddy who lives only a few miles from here. He's invited both of us to see his garden Thursday evening. Is that all right with you?"

My first thought was, *heavens no.* I don't want to spend an hour walking around some guy's garden, and I don't care how cool his blog is. I'm sure he's done interesting things in his garden, but I have other things I'd rather do.

But my next thought was, if I never stretched out of my comfort zone, I'd read and write all the time, with an occasional movie or sports event on the side. Thanks to my wife, who is very different from me, my life is much richer.

So I smiled and said, "Sure. That'll be fine."

That evening we spent the better part of an hour walking through this fellow's garden. It was interesting to see how a different mind does different things with the same challenges we face. Also, it turned out he had a Ph.D. in English and is the most interesting man I've met since becoming a Texan 18 years ago.

My wife and I share a lot of things in common. We have identical worldviews, and we share a love of the arts, literature, and writing. Also, we have our differences. She needs an active social life. I need peace and quiet, and time to myself. She has a practically endless desire to learn more about earthly delights: birds, butterflies, flowers, trees, fish, food, and wine. I'm more of a philosopher. So, my life expands when she pulls me into her world, and her life expands when I share my ideas with her.

This sort of flies in the face of highly publicized dating services with their personality assessments. Their approach to compatibility is to help you find someone who is a lot like you. They believe it will increase the chances that you'll get along. The problem is, in the long haul, you need a lot more in a relationship than commonalities to get along.

I'll tell you this: If I had to live with someone like me, there would be few conflicts, but I wouldn't want to spend the rest of my life with someone who has the same limitations as I do.

To me, the smart money is to establish relationships with people with whom you have key common ground but who aren't like you in many ways. Then, refuse to be annoyed by the differences. Instead, accept them for what they are—unique, valuable ways of being. Affirm the differences, celebrate them, learn from them, and make use of them. If you open your mind and heart when you're with people who aren't like you, they'll share insights and solutions you'd never consider on your own. They'll introduce you to joys in life that would otherwise be lost to you. They'll help make you a whole person.

It isn't always easy to appreciate people who are different from you. Humanity is very diverse. When you think of all the ways individuals can be different—personality, culture, education, life experience, religion, economic status, skills, knowledge, values, attitudes, interests, and relationships—it seems obvious that no two people on the planet are alike. Some can be radically different from you. When someone doesn't think like you or act like you, it can be hard to communicate and connect. The other person might do things that surprise you or even shock you. You'll find that you disagree about a lot of things. It could be a stretch to like such a person. You'd probably rather spend time with someone more like you.

Years ago, I consulted with a group of trainers. I had expertise in creative problem-solving, and they were teaching a week-long course on that topic. From time to time, I would go to their facility to help them with their program.

It was always strange because all five people in that group were unlike me in the same way. Each of them was spontaneous, playful, and outgoing. They had wonderful charisma and were a great asset for presenting training. I, on the other hand, am logical, intellectual, serious, realistic, and goal-directed. For them, each day was a kind of party, and it was a stretch for me to fit in with that group. They valued my participation because I evaluated their program, got things organized, and kept them on schedule. I also taught the sessions on decision-making, a topic they didn't enjoy.

In short, we appreciated, valued, and used our differences. But I often thought it would be wise if they hired team members with more diversity instead of favoring people so much like themselves, with whom they connected so magically.

I think the lesson of appreciation goes something like this: That so many people aren't like you is good news, not bad news. It's good news because you're not all things. You have your strengths, but you aren't strong in all areas. You know a lot, but you certainly don't know everything. You have your focus and your individuality, and you want to be valued for that. You want your talents to be well used. And people who aren't like you feel the same way. They have a lot to contribute, and you can benefit from that if you do two hard things.

One, get acquainted with these people. Hire them. Learn how to team with them. Spend more time with them, even though it would be easier and less of a challenge to associate with people who are like you.

Two, appreciate the differences. And as a part of your appreciation, value them. Affirm them. Learn from them. Make the best use of their strengths. It will be a stretch, but making your life experience more diverse will enrich you and complete you.

What is APPRECIATION?

Appreciation begins with accepting that people are different from each other, valuing these differences, and making the best use of this diversity—because everyone is bringing something unique to the party. You accept and respect that people have a right to their diverse backgrounds, perspectives, and values. Instead of reacting negatively to the contrary opinions, beliefs, or behaviors of others, you discover how to relate constructively, make use of their strengths, and get the work done.

Why appreciation is important:

If you work around other people, you'll need mutually supportive and beneficial relationships that allow you to cooperate and collaborate—regardless of how different they are from you and everyone else. You not only need to coexist peacefully, but you also need to rely on them and make the best use of what they have to offer. Otherwise, you won't succeed. Respectful communication and a free exchange of ideas are important to your success.

"It does me no injury for my neighbor to say there are 20 gods, or no god. It neither picks my pocket nor breaks my leg."

Thomas Jefferson, American president

What you can do to strengthen your appreciation:

- ✓ Stand up for the rights of others to practice their own religion in their own way or even to have no religion at all.

- ✓ Learn about different cultural practices, traditions, and customs.
- ✓ Engage in respectful dialogue with people who have differing opinions in order to understand their perspectives.
- ✓ Treat people equally regardless of their race, ethnicity, gender identity, or sexual orientation.
- ✓ Show acceptance for lifestyles that are different from your own, including such things as relationships, clothing choices, dietary preferences, etc.
- ✓ Spend more time with someone you know who is very different from you.
- ✓ Identify someone who has a very different background and talk with them simply to discover more about them. You don't have to agree with anything they say. Just listen and learn.

Appreciation is a behavior pattern. The more you practice it, the stronger it will become. Along the way, you can expect both successes and disappointments. So partner with someone to coach you with encouragement; then learn from your attempts, stick with it, and you'll get stronger over time.

"If civilization is to survive, we must cultivate the science of human relationships—the ability of all peoples, of all kinds, to live together, in the same world at peace."

Franklin D. Roosevelt, American president

Learn from people who aren't like you, and your mind will expand.

"Darkness cannot drive out darkness; only light can do that. Hate cannot drive out hate; only love can do that."

Martin Luther King, Jr., American civil rights leader

"Forgiveness means it finally becomes unimportant that you hit back. You're done. But it doesn't necessarily mean that you want to have lunch with the person."

Anne Lamott, American novelist

"To err is human, to forgive, divine."

Alexander Pope, British poet

"If we practice an eye for an eye and a tooth for a tooth, soon the whole world will be blind and toothless."

Mohandas Gandhi, Indian religious leader

16

Forgiveness

Anger and resentment keep you focused on the past. Let it go and move on.

Dr. Josef Mengele was the evil German SS medical officer known as the "Angel of Death" at the Auschwitz concentration camp during World War II. The purpose of the camp was to implement Hitler's "Final Solution." Jews and other people deemed undesirable were brought there by trains, and thousands were killed every day.

Mengele was a cold-blooded mass murderer. He met the trains and selected people for his grisly medical experiments. One of his pet projects was doing experimental medical procedures on sets of twins, such as testing the effects of germ and chemical warfare agents. At the conclusion of each experiment, he killed the children and performed comparative autopsies on them. He tortured about 1,500 sets of twins. Only about 100 pairs of twins survived.

I had the good fortune to meet Eva Kor, one of the survivors, at a public speaking event. Eva, not quite five feet tall, is a highly energetic, articulate, and straightforward woman with a rich sense of humor. She has made it her life's work to spread a message of peace and humanity to the world.

Her presentation had two parts. The second part was her story of how she came to forgive the Nazis, including Josef Mengele, the man who tortured and abandoned her to die.

But first, she described what happened to her at the camp, which helped people understand the magnitude of what she forgave. No doubt you've heard the stories and seen the films about the horror of the death camps. The reality was much worse than that. If you want to know about it, I encourage you to get a copy of Eva Kor's book, *Surviving the Angel of Death: The Story of a Mengele Twin in Auschwitz.* By her account, she survived simply because she refused to die.

How she came to forgive Mengele and her other tormentors is an interesting story. She said that she was asked to speak to a group of doctors at Boston College. They asked her if she could bring one of the Nazi doctors with her. She didn't even know if any of the doctors were still alive, but the request intrigued her. So she checked and found one living in Germany. In 1993, she visited him. To her surprise, the man treated her with humility, kindness, and respect. When she asked him if he knew what was happening at Auschwitz, he said, "This is the nightmare I live with," and described how the Jews were killed. He didn't want to go with her to speak, but he agreed to sign a document.

Eva wanted to thank the doctor, but she didn't know how to do it. Ultimately, she decided to write him a letter of forgiveness. It took her four months to write it, and in it, she forgave everyone who had ever hurt her. She even forgave herself for her hard feelings toward her parents. She even forgave Hitler.

It wasn't easy to do this. For one thing, the other surviving twins were angry with her. They misunderstood, thinking that Eva's gesture put a favorable light on the Nazis. But Eva experienced a surprising personal benefit. In her own words:

"I believe with every fiber of my being that every person has the human right to live with or without the pain of the past and that it is a personal choice. My question is, how many people would choose to live with pain when they could heal from it?

"I believe that this healing is possible through forgiveness, and I believe in forgiveness as the ultimate act of self-healing and self-empowerment. Once a person decides to forgive, there is a tremendous feeling of wholeness in thought, spirit, and action, all moving in the same direction, creating a powerful force for healing and freedom.

"My forgiving the Nazis is a gift of freedom I gave myself, a gift of peace for myself. It is also a gift of peace for everybody who wants it. Both peace and war begin in the heart and mind. Pain and anger are the seeds of war. Forgiveness is the seed of peace.

"When one human being harms another, the perpetrator lives with the burden of guilt. To atone, they can admit responsibility, resolve never to do it again, make restitution, apologize, and ask for forgiveness. When the victim expresses forgiveness, some of that burden may be lifted.

"Whether the guilty one does any of these things, the victim experiences a burden as well. It's the burden of pain and anger. The only thing that can lift this burden is forgiveness. Forgiveness is something you do for yourself. It's an act of self-healing, self-liberation, and self-empowerment. What was done no longer defines who I am. I let go of anger and bitterness.

"It takes strength to forgive. You decide to stop nurturing hate, resentment, bitterness, and other bad feelings about what happened. When you do, the burden is lifted from your heart and mind. What happened in the past stops being a part of your present and your future. You walk away from the incident, leaving it in the past.

"I have no more nightmares. I can talk about it, and I can joke about it, and it doesn't bother me."

A great many people still think that when you forgive someone, you're doing something for the other person. Yes, the person who harmed you may regret doing it and may have asked for forgiveness. Indeed, telling the person that you forgive them may give them some psychological relief from feelings of guilt.

But the primary beneficiary is the person who forgives. As a friend of mine told me, "To forgive means not dwelling on past hurts or pains, which can torture one's own spirit." When you decide to stop reliving the hurt, when you commit to leaving the past in the past and let go of feelings of anger, vengeance, resentment, hate, and other corrosive emotions, a great burden is lifted.

What is FORGIVENESS?

It's natural to feel anger or resentment when someone has caused you distress, pain, or harm. However, continuing to foster these feelings can undermine relationships and your personal well-being. Instead, forgiveness—intentionally letting go of negative feelings—can free you from the weight of carrying a grudge or seeking retribution. You can forgive without forgetting, even without communicating your forgiveness.

Why forgiveness is important:

Family conflicts can arise due to inconsideration, inheritances, favoritism, or past hurts. In a neighborhood, bothersome noise, property disputes, and other conflicts can promote long-standing ill will. Rivalries can keep people from working together. The result is that people continue to resent each other without seeking a resolution. But lasting anger or resentment is an emotional burden. Releasing negative feelings can allow you to break free from the burden of negativity, refashion relationships, and find personal healing and peace.

"Anger is an acid that can do more harm to the vessel in which it is stored than to anything on which it is poured."

Mark Twain, American novelist

What you can do to strengthen your forgiveness:

- ✓ Recall a situation where you felt anger towards a close friend because of something they said or did. Decide to let go of your resentment. Understanding that everyone makes mistakes, you can choose to rebuild trust.
- ✓ If someone who has wronged you subsequently expresses genuine remorse, forgive the person and work to repair the damaged relationship.
- ✓ At work, if a colleague takes credit for your work and you confront them about it, and if they sincerely apologize and acknowledge their mistake, put it behind you and rebuild a positive working relationship.
- ✓ You can also forgive yourself. Suppose you made a significant mistake that caused harm to yourself or others. After taking responsibility for your actions and reflecting on the situation, you can move on from the guilt by accepting your mistake, learning from the experience, and committing to personal growth.
- ✓ No one is perfect. If a friend has been doing something that disturbs you, give some encouraging feedback so you can move past your negative feelings.
- ✓ If something happened a long time ago and it still bothers you, consider that you have carried the resentment too long and put the past in the past.
- ✓ You don't have to continue a hurtful relationship. You can exercise forgiveness and move on from both the pain and the relationship.

It may not be easy to let go of a past hurt. But keep working on it until you don't care about it anymore. To help you move on, talk about your efforts with a trusted friend, someone who will encourage you.

"I will permit no man to narrow and degrade my soul by making me hate him."

Booker T. Washington, American educator

Carrying a grudge is a heavy burden, with no payoff at the end.

"I do not ask the wounded person how he feels, I myself become the wounded person."

Walt Whitman, American poet

"You never really understand a person until you consider things from his point of view, until you climb inside of his skin and walk around in it."

Harper Lee, American novelist

"Empathy represents the foundation skill for all the social competencies important for work."

Daniel Goleman, American author

"Empathy is seeing with the eyes of another, listening with the ears of another, and feeling with the heart of another."

Alfred Adler, Austrian psychotherapist

17

Empathy

What others are thinking and feeling—a momentous discovery.

One day while thinking about my mother, who passed away twenty years ago, I realized that I had accidentally exercised empathy with a breakthrough result.

My mother was the kind of person who led with her emotions. In her later years, she certainly had enough aches, pains, challenges, and adversity to complain about. I tried to stay in touch (I lived in Florida, and she lived in Kansas), so I would call her at least once a week. I found these conversations difficult because I hated listening to self-pity. I didn't like thinking of her as a negative person, a whiner.

"These medications aren't working. My new doctor won't give me phenobarbital. He says he's afraid I'll get addicted."

"You don't want to get addicted. Maybe he's right."

"But this new stuff isn't helping me. I'm in pain constantly. I can't even sleep at night."

"Maybe you need to give it a chance. Sometimes, you have to use a med for a while before it starts to take effect."

"You don't understand. My life is miserable."

I would struggle to be helpful, but no matter what I said, it seemed to make her feel worse. I'd wrap up our conversation, but I had the persistent feeling that it was impossible to have a pleasant talk with my mother.

One day, I just gave up trying to be reasonable and helpful. I decided I would play along and agree with anything she said.

"You know, you're the only one who calls me. Three of my children live right here in town. They don't call, and they don't visit. Nobody cares about me anymore."

"You love your kids, so it must feel awful when you don't hear from them."

"I know how busy they are. But I wish they would just say hello once in a while."

"It would be so nice to hear from them more often."

"I know they haven't forgotten me. Charlie's on the road a lot, and Jill works day and night in her business. And Jack brings work home from the VA."

"They have busy lives. But you know they care about you."

"Maybe I should give them a call."

"You can be the one to make contact."

Instead of offering solutions and trying to get her to break through her self-pity, I just expressed empathy as I listened. The effect was miraculous. I realized she felt alone with her issues and just wanted someone to appreciate how she felt.

After that, I continued with this strategy, and our painful conversations transformed into positive, sharing ones. Now, many years after she's been gone, I realize that I was exercising the skill of expressing empathy.

Even the people we're close to—our spouse, our child, our close friends, our coworkers—are separated from us by the impossibility of following every step of their journey, of the inability always to know their thoughts and feelings. The best we can do is imagine what they are experiencing, thinking, and feeling at any given moment. When we do, this is enough.

The first step to exercising empathy is to be fully present with the people around you. This means a lot more than noticing. To achieve the kind of awareness implied in mindfulness, you can't be thinking about something that happened, about what you hope for or expect. You must experience what's in front of you—right here, right now. Your connections are most real and intense when you're able to experience people without the filter of whatever may be going on in your mind, without judging or reacting. Mindfulness makes empathy possible. You sense who people really are and what they're experiencing, not who you think they are or who you want them to be.

What is EMPATHY?

Empathy is the ability to sense other people's emotions, coupled with the ability to imagine what they might be thinking or feeling. Most of the time, we perceive the world around us, including the people in it, as entities separate from us. When you exercise empathy, you focus intensely on someone else. You shift from a self-centered perspective to appreciate someone else's feelings, thoughts, and experiences. When you express your empathy, people "feel felt."

This ability to reach out goes beyond sympathy, which involves caring about someone. In the most intense kind of empathy, you not only recognize what someone else is feeling but also imagine that you feel it yourself. You can focus your empathy on any living being. Healthy empathy doesn't make you actually feel someone else's pain; you balance your empathy with self-care.

Why empathy is important:

Sensing and acknowledging what's really going on with other people helps you act appropriately with them, thus strengthening your ability to help them and nurture relationships. You magnify your ability to relate to others. If you never exercised empathy, people might think of you as a cold or aloof person who doesn't show interest in them, which would limit your ability to lead or to be an effective team member.

"When you show deep empathy towards others, their defensive energy goes down, and their positive energy replaces it."

Stephen Covey, American author

What you can do to strengthen your empathy:

- ✓ When someone you know is going through a difficult time, listen without interrupting or offering advice until you understand what they're feeling.
- ✓ When you sense that someone is in distress, offer understanding, comfort, and encouragement.
- ✓ If you notice that a coworker is struggling with a heavy workload, offer to help.
- ✓ To acknowledge what someone is experiencing, express your understanding and acceptance of their feelings, even if they differ from your own.
- ✓ Focus on a stranger with empathy, then offer a helping hand or perform a random act of kindness.
- ✓ Keep in mind that life can be challenging for anyone. Be on the lookout for people who may be feeling distressed.
- ✓ When you notice someone is struggling, ask how they're doing and listen to understand.
- ✓ When someone behaves emotionally, describe what you sense they are feeling.

Remember that empathy is a behavior pattern. The more you practice it, the stronger it will become. Along the way, you can expect both successes and disappointments. So partner with someone to coach you with encouragement; then learn from your attempts, stick with it, and you'll get stronger over time.

"When you start to develop your powers of empathy and imagination, the whole world opens up to you."

Susan Sarandon, American actor

If humans can walk on the moon, they can walk in each other's shoes.

"My brain and my heart are my temples. My true religion is kindness."

Dalai Lama, Tibetan religious leader

"Peace begins with a smile."

Mother Teresa, Albanian-Indian Catholic nun

"Kindness begets kindness."

Sophocles, Greek playwright

"Three things in human life are important. The first is to be kind. The second is to be kind. And the third is to be kind."

Henry James, American novelist

18

Compassion

Bring light into someone's life, and your day will brighten.

When my wife told me that she was going to present a garden club program to our community on plants that attract hummingbirds, she added, "I'd like you to be there."

Now, I don't usually attend these meetings. I'm not a gardener. I can't even remember the names of the plants in our yard. My role is to dig holes and lift heavy bags of compost for the real gardener in the family. And pull weeds. I'm glad we have a garden club; it adds to the overall quality of life where I live. I'd rather read a book or watch a good movie than go to one of those meetings.

But my brain kicked in and helped me out. I asked myself why she wanted me to be there. I imagined how much work it would take for her to find all the photos and put them into a PowerPoint presentation. And it was summer; many families take vacation trips. What if she went to all that trouble and only a few people showed up?

I concluded that she not only wanted to have an impact, but she also wanted her good work to be appreciated. Since I care about my wife's feelings, I resolved to go, help her in any way I could, and give her positive feedback afterward.

And that's what I did. She gave a wonderful presentation. Her delivery was interesting and enthusiastic, and the pictures were a great help. As we left the clubhouse, I told her so. I could see that she was pleased. What a terrible mistake it would have been to make excuses and skip the meeting. I had let compassion guide me to do the right thing.

To understand our capacity for compassion, it's useful to consider the case of the psychopath, who never feels it. According to brain scientists, witnessing someone's pain or horror triggers the amygdala, a component of the emotional area of the brain. Its function is to react to threatening situations, triggering emotions such as fear or anxiety. So when we witness distress, we feel it ourselves. This empathy is the beginning of compassion. In the brain of the psychopath, the amygdala is defective. They may see someone in pain, but they don't feel it themselves. So they can perform acts of cruelty to get what they want, and it doesn't bother them.

Another area of the brain plays a part in compassion. The prefrontal cortex is the part of the brain that "understands" what is perceived, relates cause and effect, and creates plans and intentions. It is directly connected to the amygdala. In other words, it can tell the amygdala to stop generating alarm emotions. This is a good thing if the intellect determines that there's no problem. However, it can also cause someone to be insensitive to the pain of others for whatever reason.

So, compassion seems to be innate, at least for people who have a normal amygdala. When we see someone in distress, we feel distress. When we see someone in pain, we are sensitive to their pain. This natural reaction can be disrupted if the intellect intervenes and the feeling is dismissed or rationalized, resulting in no action being taken. Or, as in my case, it could present perfectly good reasons for not going to the garden club meeting.

Maybe our hard-wiring to be empathetic is why the concept of compassion permeates our language: empathy, sympathy, warmth, gentleness, tenderness, caring, kindness, consideration, thoughtfulness, concern, humanity, benevolence, and other terms. It's even a moral imperative, a core aspect of most of the world's religions.

Compassion is at the core of human relations. Imagine what it would be like if everyone you knew were cold and disinterested. All of the so-called people skills—listening, encouraging, coaching, conflict resolution, dialogue, feedback, etc.—would be far less effective if practiced without compassion.

Probably the most common barrier to compassion is the fact that we can be distracted by our own troubles. Life is full of disappointments. To protect yourself from additional pain, you could ignore the needs of others. At the other extreme, you might fly into a rage when things don't go the way you hoped. You could lash out at others when you're frustrated. Either reaction will create distance between you and others.

Despite life's inevitable hurts, you can decide to remain caring and sensitive. Thoughtful people care about the impact they have on others, and they act accordingly, regardless of how difficult their own lives are. They don't knowingly inflict harm. They control their reactions to make sure they don't hurt the people around them. They make a point of being helpful, patient, and understanding.

What is COMPASSION?

Compassion involves feelings of sympathy, caring, and empathy for the difficulties or distress of others. You acknowledge the pain, struggles, or challenges they're facing and do what you can to offer comfort, assistance, or support. You take a non-judgmental attitude, draw on your concerns, and offer to help someone through a hard time. At its best, compassion isn't narrowly focused; you can reach out not only to friends and family but also to strangers and animals.

Why compassion is important:

An important truth: it's hard to deal with the many, often unexpected challenges of life. No one gets a free pass. Every person you relate to—family, friends, coworkers, customers, even strangers—has a mixed bag of hardships to deal with. Acts of compassion can lighten their burden. At work, underlying difficulties can rob people of motivation and degrade their performance. If you're sensitive to their struggles, you can do things to support them that will strengthen relationships and motivate them to continue giving their best efforts.

"Tenderness and kindness are not signs of weakness and despair, but manifestations of strength and resolution."

Khalil Gibran, Lebanese poet

What you can do to strengthen your compassion:

- ✓ Look for opportunities to perform random acts of kindness: e.g., lend a hand to someone struggling with heavy bags, take time to give directions to a stranger who is lost, or stop to help a stranded motorist.
- ✓ Support a charitable organization, such as a homeless shelter, participate in a community cleanup, or assist in fundraising for a worthy cause.
- ✓ Support a friend who is struggling, even if it's simply being a caring listener and offering words of comfort and encouragement.
- ✓ Help disadvantaged people by advocating for fairness and equality and standing up against injustice.
- ✓ Animals need help, too. You could actively engage in rescue efforts, foster shelter pets, or support animal welfare organizations.

- ✓ Offer kindness and support for people who are grieving a loss. Express sympathy, offer practical help or simply be there, willing to listen.

To become a truly compassionate person, you need to establish it as a behavior pattern. As you consistently repeat the behavior, the brain cells involved in acts of compassion will form into circuits. Along the way, you can experience both successes and missed opportunities. If you partner with someone who will offer encouragement, you can learn from your attempts, stick with it, and get stronger over time.

"Kindness is the language which the deaf can hear and the blind can see."

Mark Twain, American novelist

Make friends before you need them, and they'll be there when you do.

"It is one of the most beautiful compensations of this life that no man can sincerely try to help another without helping himself."

Ralph Waldo Emerson, American philosopher

"Give a bowl of rice to a man and you will feed him for a day. Teach him how to grow his own rice and you will save his life."

Confucius, Chinese philosopher

"No one has ever become poor by giving."

Anne Frank, German author

"I believe we can only be truly generous when we expect nothing in return."

Muhammad Ali, American professional boxer

19

Generosity

Give with your heart, and hearts will reach out to you.

Once a controversial heavy-weight boxing champion, Muhammad Ali nicknamed himself "The Greatest." And maybe he was. After retiring from boxing, he devoted himself to humanitarian projects around the world, lending his name and celebrity presence to efforts to fight hunger and poverty. It is estimated that Ali helped feed more than 22 million people afflicted by hunger across the world. He generously shared his wealth, his time, and his considerable influence. For his efforts, he received the Presidential Medal of Freedom. His Muhammad Ali Center in Louisville focuses on peace, social responsibility, respect, and personal growth.

One of my favorite movies is "Pay It Forward," with Kevin Spacey, Helen Hunt, and Haley Joel Osment. If you've seen the movie, you know it's about generosity, perhaps the best movie ever made about this aspect of character. I've watched it a couple of times already, and I'm sure I'll want to see it again. My wife says she won't watch it because it breaks her heart. It breaks my heart, too, from beginning to end, but that doesn't stop me.

I believe generosity is a form of character strength because it's not always so easy to sense the needs of others when you have your own burdens. Disappointment, pain, and loss have a way of focusing your mind inwardly. Also, people are remarkably different from each other, which makes communication, understanding, and appreciation challenging. In most cases, other people's troubles are different from yours; you don't know what these troubles are, which makes it hard to appreciate their situation. Imperfect people act imperfectly. Sometimes they're thoughtless or careless, and the instinctive reaction is not a compassionate one. It's hard to keep in mind that this is just another human being who struggles with life and feels pain just as you do.

What is GENEROSITY?

Generosity is the willingness to give without expecting anything in return. You do it with a selfless and open-hearted attitude and a genuine concern for the well-being of others. You offer help, resources, or support to those in need. Beyond sharing material things, you can also give your time, attention, know-how, and understanding.

Why generosity is important:

No one is immune from life's unpredictable challenges. An act of kindness—even a small gesture—can make a difference. People who come to see you as caring and helpful will want to respond in kind. The relationships formed by acts of generosity can be meaningful and enduring, both in your personal life and at work.

"We make a living by what we get, but we make a life by what we give."

Winston Churchill, British prime minister and author

What you can do to strengthen your generosity:

- ✓ Donate a portion of your income to charity.
- ✓ Volunteer at a local charity or homeless shelter.
- ✓ Offer free tutoring to an underprivileged student.
- ✓ Donate blood.
- ✓ Give support to someone facing a difficult situation.
- ✓ Foster a rescued animal.
- ✓ Donate clothing, blankets, or other essential items to relief organizations.
- ✓ Help a stranger in need.
- ✓ Organize a campaign to raise funds for a worthy cause or donate time and skills to a community project, such as building homes for those in need or participating in clean-up initiatives.
- ✓ Help a coworker deal with problems or obstacles.
- ✓ Offer to help a person in need, such as someone recovering from an injury.

The more often you give, the stronger your capacity for generosity will get. While you may sometimes overlook opportunities to be generous, you can discuss your experiences with someone you trust and learn from them. Stick with it, and you'll get stronger over time.

"Never worry about numbers. Help one person at a time and always start with the person nearest you."

Mother Teresa, Albanian-Indian Catholic nun

Give what you have that's worth giving, and you will never be poor.

"People respond in accordance to how you treat them."

Nelson Mandela, South African president

"A great deal may be done by severity, more by love, but most by clear discernment and impartial justice."

Johann Wolfgang von Goethe, German poet

"The only stable state is the one in which all men are equal before the law."

Aristotle, Greek philosopher

"Seek to help all people, regardless of race, regardless of color, regardless of condition."

George Washington Carver, American scientist

20

Fairness

Create a level playing field, and winners will show up to play.

After a Sunday road trip, I was tired, and all I wanted to do was collapse in front of the TV. The only thing that interested me was a golf tournament. I don't usually follow these events, but one of my favorite players, Jim Furyk, was on top of the leaderboard going into the final hole. Good for him.

One shot behind was Brian Davis. Davis, who had never won a tournament in 16 years on the PGA tour, was ranked somewhere below 100th in the world. Now, he had a chance to do something wonderful for his career. I was sucking on my beer and starting to get interested.

Both golfers hit good drives and put their second shots on the green. Furyk's putt just missed the hole, and he settled for par. But then Davis holed a 16-footer for a birdie, and the two were tied at the end of the tournament. It was a sudden-death playoff!

The two golfers played the 18th hole again. Brian Davis's second shot hit the green in nearly the same spot as before, but shockingly, it bounced off the green, down onto some rocks, landing in hard-packed sand covered with thatch. A horrible lie! Furyk's second shot wasn't much better. It rolled off the back of the green. With his putter, Furyk lagged his third shot close to the hole, practically guaranteeing a par.

To equal that, Davis would have to hit a nearly impossible shot out of the mess off the green. Unfortunately, his ball stopped 30 feet beyond the hole. But he still had a chance. If he made the long putt, he could force another playoff hole. A million dollars hung in the balance.

But here's what happened next, and this is why I'm writing about this relatively obscure golf tournament. Brian Davis called an official over to tell him that he thought he saw something out of the corner of his eye when he took his shot. He thinks he might have touched a piece of thatch. If there is a videotape, can they check to be sure?

You see, it's against the rules to move or disturb debris before striking the ball. Doing so is considered "improving the lie of the ball," and the penalty is two strokes.

The officials reviewed the videotape in slow motion, and sure enough, the club moved a piece of thatch about an inch during the backswing. Davis was assessed two penalty strokes, which made it impossible for him to force another tie. Furyk won the tournament.

The infraction was almost invisible, unintentional, inconsequential, and no one noticed it but Davis. *But he called the infraction on himself, even though he knew it would cost him dearly*. So, after 16 years, he still hasn't won a tournament, and he's still ranked close to 100th in the world.

Brian Davis was disappointed about losing, but he had no regrets about the penalty. He did what he was supposed to do, which is very likely what Furyk would have done in the same situation. The standard of ethics in professional golf is amazingly high. It's a gentleman's game.

But Brian Davis is no longer obscure. He knows he did the right thing, and so does the entire world. His action was spotlighted by live television and has since been commented on by hundreds of sports announcers and writers. He is now a highly visible symbol of what it means to play fair.

Do you know what it feels like to be treated unfairly? I'm not talking about life. There's nothing fair about life. The world doesn't exist to make sure good things happen to you. I'm talking about other people doing the right thing so that you and others have the same opportunity to get what you're working for. Of course, after that, it's up to you. Someone else might want it more, act more decisively, prepare better, and so on. If someone else gets what you want, you can't feel bad if they play by the rules.

Life isn't a game. But in most cultures, there are expectations, norms, procedures, rules, and yes, even laws to ensure that no one has an unfair advantage. Where these guidelines are absent, others can take advantage of you. And I suppose yes, then life can seem unfair.

It hurts to be dealt with unfairly. It can hurt financially, but it will definitely wound your spirit. If you don't have an equal chance, why try?

That's what rules are for. That's why fairness matters. But mostly, it's not laws or regulations that create the kind of respect and justice we need. Mostly, it's just people who value fairness and act fairly.

When you remember Brian Davis, appreciate that it's not always easy to act fairly. As in his case, your own needs may be at stake. You may have biases or loyalties that conflict with doing the right thing. You may not want to give someone else a fair shake if you feel they don't deserve it.

But if you want to live in a world where fairness is possible, you and others have to choose to act fairly and promote fairness. Fairness won't be possible if people like you don't take responsibility for making sure that everyone has the same reasonable chance for success.

What is FAIRNESS?

Being fair means being just, equitable, and impartial. It means giving everyone equal opportunities, rights, and treatment. Fairness is a fundamental principle in legal systems, workplaces, educational institutions, social relationships, and governance. In an organization, fairness means people are given a fair hearing and the chance to present their views or grievances. Also, opportunities, resources, rewards, and benefits are allocated based on merit rather than politics, friendships, race, gender, religion, or socioeconomic status.

Why fairness is important:

Being fair is morally and ethically right. Everyone, including you, deserves a fair chance to succeed. People need and expect you to act impartially with them. If you fail to do so, they're likely to resent you and stop trusting you, which will render you ineffective as a leader or team member. Not only would they withhold their best efforts, but they could also leave the organization, seeking better treatment elsewhere.

"If there is anything that a man can do well, I say let him do it. Give him a chance."

Abraham Lincoln, American president

What you can do to strengthen your fairness:

- ✓ If it's within your power, give everyone an equal chance to succeed, regardless of their background, gender, race, or socioeconomic status.
- ✓ In meetings, make sure everyone has the opportunity to participate and voice their opinion.
- ✓ Support policies and procedures that afford equal opportunities for job applicants, evaluating candidates based

on their qualifications, skills, and experience rather than personal connections or biases.

- ✓ Use your influence to ensure that resources such as healthcare, education, and social services are distributed based on need.
- ✓ Volunteer to support an organization that advocates for fairness.
- ✓ Help a child by giving them a fair chance to excel.

Fairness is a way of behaving in the world. The more you exercise it, the more the skill will become a comfortable, consistent pattern for you. In your efforts to consistently act fairly, you may experience both successes and difficulties. But it's important to stick with it. So, partner with someone who will offer you encouragement while you learn from your attempts, and you'll get stronger over time.

"All virtue is summed up in dealing justly."

Aristotle, Greek philosopher

Promote fairness for everyone, and it will be there for you, too.

"Faithless is he that says farewell when the road darkens."

J. R. R. Tolkien, British novelist

"A real friend is one who walks in when the rest of the world walks out."

Walter Winchell, American journalist

"I have underlying respect for the broad-shouldered family man and woman who care more about their kids than themselves, and they are willing to make sacrifices so that their children can succeed."

Frank Borman, American astronaut

"We are all in the same boat in a stormy sea, and we owe each other a terrible loyalty."

G. K. Chesterton, British novelist

21

Loyalty

Be there for those you care about, and you'll never be alone.

In his book *Outliers,* Malcolm Gladwell attempts to explain why some people are remarkably successful. In one story, he describes Roseto, a town in Pennsylvania populated almost exclusively by immigrants from Roseto Valfortore, a small village in Italy. In the 1950s, doctors around Roseto noticed that almost no one under the age of 65 had heart disease. Also, there was almost no suicide, alcoholism, drug addiction, or crime there. In fact, the major cause of death in Roseto was *old age*. After decades of studies, researchers found that none of the usual variables made any difference: not diet, not exercise, not genetics, and not the environment.

To everyone's surprise, the evidence showed that the major contributing factor was *relationships*. "You'd see three-generational family meals, all the bakeries, the people walking up and down the street, sitting on their porches talking to each other, the blouse mills where the women worked during the day, while the men worked in the slate quarry. It was magical." They had transplanted their unique Italian village culture to create a close-knit community of caring relationships. That, far more than anything else, caused them to live long, healthy lives.

One force that strengthens relationships is a dynamic we refer to as *loyalty*. But what is meant by that, exactly?

Our company has a great relationship with our bank, one that has endured more than 30 years of high-flying and free-falling recession economies. A practical and personable businessman, our banker has been loyal to us all this time. His most recent act of loyalty was to restructure our credit to our advantage to help us thrive during a recession. He did this on his own initiative, even though it involved some risk to his bank. Naturally, we've been loyal to him, too.

So loyalty is earned, and it's a two-way street. Being loyal means giving a relationship a higher priority. Simple enough—if you care about someone, then be there for them. Be true to them. Watch their back. Do what's in their best interests. Based on your choices, a relationship will grow—or atrophy. The problem is that most people have many loyalties, including loyalty to themselves. And loyalties can sometimes conflict with each other. So it may be hard to choose one over the other.

Sometimes, loyalty to a friend can conflict with loyalty to a principle.

More than 50 years ago, when I was an advisor in Vietnam, I was on a sweep through the countryside north of Cu Chi. On this occasion, I was riding on top of a U.S. Army mechanized infantry assault vehicle next to an old friend who was the commander of an infantry company. On that day, we had teamed up for a joint mission—my Vietnamese counterpart's infantry platoon and Butch's mechanized infantry company. All the soldiers rode on top of the vehicles instead of inside in case one of them hit a booby trap. Together, we hunted for the Viet Cong.

Actually, the Viet Cong were smart enough to hear the loud vehicles coming a mile away and hide until we passed. So Butch had arranged for a Cobra helicopter gunship to fly ahead of us, looking for anything suspicious. Mid-morning, my friend got a call from the chopper that a "suspect" was running away in an open field. The pilot asked for permission to open fire.

"How do you know he's an enemy?" I asked Butch.

He smiled at me. "The friendlies don't try to run away."

"That's not always true. You need more info."

Instead, he gave the order for the pilot to engage him. Immediately, we heard the long, loud burst of the mini-gun. Butch then gave the order for his company to check the area ahead for more enemy forces.

We came through the trees to witness a scene I'll never forget. The Cobra's accuracy had been deadly. A man's body lay in the middle of an open field. A young boy came running, screaming and crying. By the time I got off the vehicle, the boy was crying over his father. When I removed the man's ID card from his shirt pocket, it was covered with blood. But it confirmed that the man was a local farmer, not the enemy at all.

A terrible mistake had been made. The life of an innocent man had been ended. It shouldn't have happened. It was the result of an impulsive, callous decision. I felt certain that the boy's sorrow would transform into hatred, and he would eventually join the Viet Cong. We hadn't destroyed an enemy; we had created one.

This incident bothered me. I felt conflicted. Should I remain loyal to my friend? Or did valuing human life and humane treatment represent a higher loyalty? Later that week, I reported my friend to the authorities. It was a hard call, one that had repercussions. My friend was relieved of his command, a consequence that ruined his career. He and I never communicated again after that. Forty years later, I learned that he became the CFO of a big company and a benefactor in his community.

For me, this experience had a hard lesson—that loyalty is an issue in every relationship and that loyalty decisions are sometimes hard to make. Also, it's easy to make bad choices, especially if you aren't sensitive to the element of loyalty in a particular relationship.

What is LOYALTY?

Loyalty means being faithful in your relationship to a person, cause, organization, or belief. You reliably support and stand by someone or something in both favorable and challenging circumstances. Based on the bond you have with the object of your loyalty, you defend its interests and work towards its success and well-being. If needed, you sacrifice time, resources, or personal interests to remain faithful and dedicated.

Why loyalty is important:

Loyalty is a binding element in all relationships. In an organization, leadership, and team cooperation are founded on loyalty. It works both ways: people take care of each other; they have each other's backs. When someone is disloyal in any way, the bond is fractured.

"I entirely appreciate loyalty to one's friends, but loyalty to the cause of justice and honor stands above it."

Theodore Roosevelt, American president

What you can do to strengthen your loyalty:

- ✓ With your friends, offer support, maintain confidentiality, and stand up for them.
- ✓ If you have a life partner, remain faithful and trustworthy in your actions and support their well-being and happiness.
- ✓ As an employee, work to achieve the organization's success, even during difficult times.

- ✓ Work collaboratively with your team, supporting team goals more than individual achievements.
- ✓ Express loyalty to your values by standing up for what you believe in.
- ✓ When a friend is going through a hard time, offer support and help.
- ✓ The next time you buy your favorite product, make a mental note of why you're still loyal to it.

Loyalty is a behavior pattern. The more you practice it, the easier it will become to make the right call. Along the way, you may experience both successes and disappointments. You can learn valuable lessons from both. Partner with someone you can talk to about your attempts, someone who will encourage and help you stick with it so you get stronger over time.

"In the end, we will not remember the words of our enemies, but the silence of our friends."

Martin Luther King, Jr., American civil rights leader

When times are hard, you'll find out who is loyal and who is not.

"Trust is the glue of life. It's the most essential ingredient in effective communication. It's the foundational principle that holds all relationships."

Stephen Covey, American author

"It is prudent never to trust wholly those who have deceived us even once."

Rene Descartes, French mathematician

"The toughest thing about the power of trust is that it's very difficult to build and very easy to destroy."

Thomas J. Watson, Sr., American business leader

"Do not trust all men, but trust men of worth; the former course is silly, the latter a mark of prudence."

Democritus, Greek philosopher

22

Trust

Once betrayal is discovered, trust will be lost in an instant.

All I Need to Know I Learned from My Cat, by Suzy Becker, is a fun read, especially if you love cats. Apparently, two million owners of the book agree.

I've lived with cats for 50 years, and I find them to be wonderful companions who often behave in an exemplary manner. I've often thought of them as good examples of some of the personal strengths I describe in this book.

My cat Ernest was a role model for trust. Every mid-morning, he came to my desk and rolled onto his back so I could pet his tummy. Most cats are wary about being petted this way, but this behavior pattern rewards both the human and the cat. When visitors met Ernest, their typical reaction was, "I think I'll take this one home." This affectionate interchange with Ernest was based on trust. He allowed himself to be vulnerable, and his reward was his favorite form of affection.

Of course, trust is earned. He trusted me because I always gave him what he needed. I was careful not to frighten him or hurt him. I'm not sure Earnest had thought this through, but the truth is, he was taking a risk. There was always a chance that someone could rub him the wrong way.

The lesson: Sometimes, you have to trust people to get what you want. Thank you, Ernest.

I guess I'm trusting you now to accept that I'm not being flip when I use a story about my cat to illustrate an important principle in human relations.

Trust isn't always so easy to give. That's why it's considered a character skill. When you think about it, you need to trust that:

- Your friends will remain loyal.
- Your coworkers will pull their fair share of the work.
- Others will do what they say they'll do.
- The person talking to you is telling you the truth.
- The things you buy are well-made and will function as advertised.
- The people you pay to fix things will actually do that.
- The personal information you reveal to others will be kept confidential.
- People who share the road with you will drive safely.

You have to trust people because there are no guarantees about what will happen. You never know for sure what others are thinking or feeling, how they'll react, or the impact of their actions. Sometimes, the risk of being disappointed is small, and trust is easy. But sometimes, a lot is at stake. You may be reluctant to trust someone, even if the individual has earned it.

I once coached a manager who had a hard time trusting members of his team. During my first visit with him, I noticed that about 20 pink call-back slips were neatly arranged on his desk. He explained that he made a lot of calls; it was his way of staying on top of things. Our conversation was interrupted three times by such calls.

When I talked with his staff, they said he checked on them repeatedly throughout the day. He asked about every detail of every task for which they were responsible. He wanted things done a certain way, and this was how he made this happen. They complained that responding to his phone calls took time away from work and hindered their productivity. It also eroded their morale. They had talent and experience, and they wanted to be trusted to do their jobs. According to them, they had earned his trust, but he seemed reluctant to give it. He was a micromanager.

Trust is a two-way street. Yes, managers need to trust their team members, but also employees need to trust that their managers will do the right things to make them successful. Managers earn this trust by leading effectively, being genuine and loyal, and making ethical decisions. Any breach of integrity, no matter how small, can create distrust. For example, what if a manager routinely includes small personal expenses on his travel reimbursement vouchers? If employees find out that he does this, they may wonder what else he will do.

Trust is essential for healthy relationships, and we should treat it as the precious commodity it is. Trust involves risk, but you can't live a fulfilling life without trust.

What is TRUST?

Trust means having faith and confidence that people will act with integrity, honesty, and reliability. Over time, people will come to trust you because you consistently deliver. It works both ways: People and institutions can earn your trust through transparency and fulfillment of expectations. Trust is always earned. While trust takes time to develop, it can be quickly broken if betrayed or violated.

Why trust is important:

Trust is crucial for maintaining healthy and successful relationships. At work, leaders need to depend on others to carry out important tasks. Team members also need to depend on each other; they need to trust that others will act in each other's best interests and do what they're supposed to do.

"It is an equal failing to trust everybody, and to trust nobody."

British proverb

What you can do to strengthen your trust:

- ✓ Monitor the behavior of others through the filter of trust: Do they do what you've trusted them to do?
- ✓ When you purchase a product or service, if the business doesn't deliver what was promised, withdraw your trust and work with someone else.
- ✓ Get information about your online platforms: do they protect your personal information, provide secure transactions, and maintain privacy?
- ✓ When your children or the young people you work with aren't honest or don't make responsible decisions, discuss it with them to make it a learning experience.
- ✓ In traffic, carefully watch the actions of other drivers: are they careful and considerate?
- ✓ Hold elected officials accountable for acting in the public's best interest and fulfilling their promises.
- ✓ When someone you trust has failed to meet your expectations, instead of immediately cutting them off, give them constructive feedback and a chance to remedy the situation.

- ✓ "Trust but verify." Extend your trust consciously. Do at least some minimal checking.
- ✓ When you trust someone to do something important for you, tell them you are doing so: I trust that you'll be able to do this for me.

Trust is a behavior pattern. The more you practice it, the easier it will become to trust appropriately. To learn from your experiences with trust, share what you've learned with someone who will encourage you and help you stick with it.

"If someone betrays you once, it is his fault; if he betrays you twice, it is your fault."

Eleanor Roosevelt, American diplomat

Let trust be earned, and you'll rarely be disappointed.

"There are no problems we cannot solve together, and very few we can solve by ourselves."

Lyndon Johnson, American president

"People want to be on a team. They want to be part of something bigger than themselves. They want to feel that they are doing something for the greater good."

Mike Krzyzewski, American college basketball coach

"United we stand, divided we fall."

Aesop, Greek storyteller

"By working together, pooling our resources, and building on our strengths, we can accomplish great things."

Ronald Reagan, American president

23

Cooperation

Add your hands to the hands of others, and you'll move the big rock.

I enjoy working alone. In fact, I work at my computer in isolation all day long. But that fact is misleading. I coordinate my work dozens of times a day with my coworkers through email, texting, and phone.

As I reflect on my life so far, I have to say that everything I've accomplished has been the result of a team effort. In fact, it's hard to think of an example of anything noteworthy that's accomplished strictly by an individual effort. I know it happens, but it's certainly the exception.

I hear this all the time: *You can get what you want by helping other people get what they want.* Author Brian Tracy put it this way: "Teamwork is so important that it is virtually impossible for you to reach the heights of your capabilities or make the money that you want without becoming very good at it."

But not all groups enjoy good teamwork. Each person has personal goals and wants to succeed as an individual. The needs of the one can conflict with the needs of the many. With everything a person has to do, it may be challenging to keep the group perspective in mind or to stay motivated to help the other members do their best.

I'm a big fan of college basketball, and whenever I think about teamwork, the first image that comes to mind is that of five players moving in concert on a basketball court. I think of the Los Angeles Lakers in the Magic Johnson era, the Boston Celtics in the Larry Bird era, or the Chicago Bulls in the Michael Jordan era. Once I had played that movie in my mind, the principles of team performance seemed rather evident. In basketball, a team that brings superior teamwork and energy can usually defeat an opponent that has superior talent. And, of course, the combination of teamwork, energy, *and* talent is hard to beat. What does it take for a group of people to function as a "high-performing team?" Consider these questions:

- Does the group have a meaningful purpose that members can relate to?
- Have the members been assigned roles that are key to team success?
- Do the role-players do their jobs with high levels of skill and effort?
- Do they keep each other informed, share resources, and help each other when needed?
- Have they formed a bond through common effort, adversity, and achievement?

Of course, team sports are an easy example. But I'm convinced that these parameters can be applied to any group effort—even to a family.

When we moved to the Texas Hill Country, our new home had no landscaping. Our acre was covered with mud, tree shards, and construction debris. On our limestone ridge, the "soil" consisted mostly of boulders, rocks, and pebbles, with some clay mixed in. When we started, the bad news was that we were faced with two or three years of hard physical labor. The good news was that we could make it look any way we wanted. My theory was that the land would tell us what to do. And that's sort of what happened—along with some vision and planning.

That first spring, we had a lot of rain. Since our home was built on the downslope of a ridge, we watched as gullies formed in our yard. I soon realized that the land was telling us that we should transform these gullies into a dry creek bed.

To do that, we needed to deepen and widen the gullies, link them into a drainage system, and extend it for about 100 feet across our backyard. Then, we needed to gather an assortment of rocks from all over the property and place them along the edges. The final step would be to pour concrete and rocks into the base of the bed along its entire length. And, oh yeah, make it look like Mother Nature had created it.

I had just started the project when my sister-in-law came for a visit. She looked at what I had done so far and said, "You shouldn't do this by yourself. Let us help you. We can all come out next weekend, and you can tell us what to do. It will be fun."

I tried to play that movie in my mind, and my mind was blank. That's always a bad sign. But I thought if I refused her generous offer, I might hurt her feelings. So I told her, "You know, we really could use some help. Digging the trench is a lot more work than I thought it would be. If you guys can help me get that done, I can handle the rest of it."

So, the following weekend, her family showed up ready to work. We supplied gloves, pick-axes, shovels, barbecue, and cold drinks. Before long, it became clear that some of us needed to dig, some needed to gather rocks, and some needed to move dirt. Soon, we were working as a team. Everyone worked hard, and at the end of the day, the dry creek bed had been dug.

It took me about three more weeks to rearrange and embed the rocks into the sides of the gully. It was a labor of love, let me tell you.

Later, when it came time to pour the concrete, I realized I couldn't do it without help. So, as I mixed the concrete in a wheelbarrow, my wife arranged the rocks. As I poured, she quickly placed the rocks in the concrete before it dried. For days, we repeated this procedure about twenty times as we moved down the slope. A week later, the creek bed was completely dry and cured. We put in some border plants, and later, the family gathered to celebrate. We named the new feature "Webb Creek" to honor the family team effort.

What is COOPERATION?

Cooperation happens when people work together towards a common goal. It's driven by the recognition that doing so will yield better outcomes than individual or competitive approaches. Key elements of cooperation include trust, respect, and a shared understanding of roles and objectives. Individuals and their leaders prioritize sharing responsibilities, communicating effectively, and finding consensus. People in groups and organizations pool their efforts, resources, and skills to achieve mutually beneficial outcomes.

Why cooperation is important:

Achieving a team goal requires a team effort. As members perform their roles, they communicate effectively with each other. If everyone's efforts aren't in synch, they can create duplication and conflicts. Not coordinating priorities, resources, and expertise can limit others' ability to deal with problems creatively. A team could even become polarized and divided.

"If you think and achieve as a team, the individual accolades will take care of themselves. Talent wins games, but teamwork wins championships."

Michael Jordan, American professional basketball player

What you can do to strengthen your cooperation:

- ✓ In the workplace, find ways to support the work of your team members.
- ✓ As a member of your community, pool your resources with others to address common challenges, such as organizing neighborhood clean-ups, building parks, or supporting local schools.
- ✓ Ask some of the people you work with to provide you with more clarity about their roles so you can better support them.
- ✓ When you notice someone striving with a tough project, ask: *How can I help?*
- ✓ When you need help, don't be concerned about appearing weak or incompetent. Ask for it.

Facilitating a cooperative approach is a behavior pattern. The more often you make that effort, the more reinforced the pattern will get. Connect with someone to coach you with encouragement; then learn from your attempts, stick with it, and you'll get stronger over time.

"I never got far until I stopped imagining I had to do everything myself."

Frank W. Woolworth, American business leader

No one can be all things. And with a little help, you won't have to try.

"Consciously or unconsciously, every one of us does render some service or other. If we cultivate the habit of doing this service deliberately, our desire for service will steadily grow stronger, and will make, not only our own happiness, but that of the world at large."

Mohandas Gandhi, Indian political leader

"Not everybody can be famous. But everybody can be great, because greatness is determined by service."

Martin Luther King, Jr., American civil rights leader

"In every community there is work to be done. In every heart there is the power to do it."

Marianne Williamson, American author

"There is no higher religion than human service. To work for the common good is the greatest creed."

Albert Schweitzer, French philosopher

24

Service

Pay your dues with service, and enjoy the many benefits of membership.

In 1964 Martin Luther King, Jr., won the Nobel Peace Prize for his efforts to end racial discrimination. He was the youngest person ever to receive that honor. He dedicated his life to promoting civil rights in the United States. When he was assassinated in 1968, his focus had expanded to include ending poverty and the Vietnam War. A martyr and symbol for human rights, his service-oriented life is commemorated annually on Martin Luther King Day, a U.S. national holiday.

Mother Teresa was an Albanian Catholic nun who became a citizen of India. She ministered to the poor, sick, orphaned, starving, and dying. Over the years, her work expanded to 610 missions in 123 countries at the time of her death in 1997. She was beatified by the Catholic Church and is considered a likely candidate for sainthood.

It's good to have these very visible reminders about how important and fulfilling it is to be of service. But the point of mentioning icons of service—and, of course, there are many others—is not to suggest that you stop what you're doing and dedicate the rest of your life to public service. Or that you necessarily need to give more money to charity or spend more time volunteering your time and talent.

Rather, the imperative is to think about what you're doing now as a valuable form of service. Because when you do, you'll do that job even better.

I've been a manager for over 50 years now, but I didn't become fully effective as a leader until I realized it was my job to serve the people I was in charge of. I know that most managers don't think of themselves that way, but it's the most useful and realistic way to define their role. A manager's job is to contribute whatever team members need, so they can do their best work to achieve the team's mission. And employees need a lot: training, experience, inspiration, support, empowerment, and encouragement. There are over 20 million managers in the U.S. alone. If they failed to provide these leadership services to their work units, productivity would grind to a halt.

So, the concept of service needs to be broadened. Most people have service-related jobs—people in the helping professions, customer service, government service, military service, consulting, technical support, maintenance and repair, custodial services, legal services, etc.—that give them the opportunity to contribute to the well-being of others. However, every job and every role can be seen as a form of service. Coaches serve their athletes. Teachers serve their students. Parents serve their children. The attitude of service can also enrich friendships—friends contributing what's needed in a relationship and being there for the people they care about.

When you focus on what you can do for the people around you, when you think about how to help them do what they need to do, that's when good things happen.

What is SERVICE?

Service entails helping, supporting, or contributing to the needs of others. It involves a selfless attitude and a genuine desire to make a positive impact on the lives of others. In an organization, leaders serve team members by empowering them with what they need to succeed. Team members serve each other, and everyone serves customers and suppliers. Even small acts of service matter. You reach out however you can, offering help, support, and guidance. You serve from a desire to contribute to the greater good.

Why service is important:

A "service" attitude is the most appropriate way to understand how you can best work with others. When you see your interactions with others as serving them, you make a special effort to help them meet the challenges of their life or work. You give your best leadership. You give your best teamwork. A service-oriented, cooperative effort results in the highest levels of individual and collective performance.

"Service to others is the rent you pay for your room here on earth."

Muhammad Ali, American boxer

What you can do to strengthen your service:

- ✓ Make specific efforts to better serve everyone you come in contact with at work.
- ✓ Take the initiative to serve your friends or members of your family.
- ✓ Volunteer at a local food bank or homeless shelter.
- ✓ Tutor or mentor a disadvantaged child.
- ✓ Offer companionship or help to an elderly person or someone with disabilities.
- ✓ Donate blood regularly.

- ✓ Participate in community projects.
- ✓ Support disaster relief efforts.
- ✓ Provide emotional support for someone who is struggling.
- ✓ Donate funds, time, or expertise for medical research, education, or humanitarian aid.
- ✓ Perform even the smallest act of service, such as opening a door for an older person.
- ✓ Organize a service project to benefit a group of children.

There are so many ways to serve. Your goal is to establish service as a behavior pattern. The more you serve others, the stronger your desire to serve will get. Connect with a like-minded person who can join you in this process, offering encouragement to stick with it as you get stronger over time.

"Our prime purpose in this life is to help others."

Dalai Lama, Tibetan religious leader

Commit to service, and your world will be a better place to live in.

PART THREE

BUILDING A STRONGER WORK ETHIC

Hard workers don't put things off or quit when the going gets tough. They come in early and stay late to make sure important tasks are finished. Simply put, they make the needed effort and get things done. While employers love to hire and promote them, not everyone has this kind of work ethic, which is more about having the character strengths that matter for work than about being smart. In this section, I describe 12 character skills that are highly valued in the workplace and how to strengthen them:

25. Commitment
26. Responsibility
27. Accountability
28. Initiative
29. Creativity
30. Proactivity
31. Decisiveness
32. Perseverance
33. Effort
34. Excellence
35. Open-mindedness
36. Flexibility

"The person who makes a success of living is the one who sees his goal steadily and aims for it unswervingly."

Cecil B. DeMille, American movie director and producer

"There's no scarcity of opportunity to make a living at what you love. There is only a scarcity of resolve to make it happen."

Wayne Dyer, American author

"Only one who devotes himself to a cause with his whole strength and soul can be a true master. Mastery demands all of a person."

Albert Einstein, American physicist

"If you do not make a total commitment to whatever you are doing, then you start looking to bail out the first time the boat starts leaking."

Lou Holtz, American college football coach

25

Commitment

Pay full price, and what you seek will be offered to you.

I once knew this fellow who loved golf more than anything in his life. He was on the golf course two or three times a week, and as a result, he was an above-average player. It was fun to walk around with him and watch him make shots.

One day, he confided in me that he believed he could make it on the PGA tour. "I'm wasting my time in this dead-end job of mine when I could be making multiple six figures easy on the tour."

He was almost forty years old, a little old to be competing with all the young, talented players who also shared that goal. I wondered if he'd thought it through. "It sounds like a great goal," I said. "Do you know what you have to do to make it happen?"

"I need a sponsor," he said.

"Yes, that's right. All the players need sponsors. Do you know how much of a stake you'll need?"

"All I need is a couple thousand. I know a guy who'll back me."

"You might need a lot more than that. It takes more than money, right? Do you know what's involved in getting your card?"

"I'm not sure. But I know I can do it."

I was a little surprised that, given his enthusiasm, he hadn't figured out what he had to do. I encouraged him to check into it. In fact, I did his homework for him. I downloaded the information off the web and gave it to him.

At the time, there were two main ways to become a PGA Tour professional. First, you could compete in "Q-School," in which aspiring players play in a series of grueling elimination tournaments. The 30 players with the lowest scores in the final tournament were given their PGA card. Another approach was to play on the Nationwide Tour, in which the top 20 money-winners at the end of the year got their card. But to play in a Nationwide event, you had to "play your way in" by paying a fee and scoring high in a preliminary qualifying round. It's amazingly competitive. Many are called, but few are chosen.

Both Q-School and the Nationwide Tour do a good job of identifying the best of the best. These high-achievers become replacements for the lowest-ranking PGA tour professionals, who lose their exemptions. To keep their card for another year, PGA professionals have to be among the top 125 money-winners on the tour.

"Do you think you can do it?" I asked after we talked about all this.

"Yeah, man. I can do it."

"Well, in my opinion it's a long shot. But you know, it's possible," I said," Even if you're a little old. Suppose you do what it takes. Have you ever won a local club championship?"

"No, but I can do it."

"It seems to me that would be a good place to start. Work on your game. Win a couple of local championships. That way, you'll prove to yourself that you're ready to play at a higher level."

A few years later, he was no closer to achieving his goal. He just wasn't willing to work on conditioning or get coaching to improve his skills. He never did enter any of the big amateur tournaments around the state. Apparently, when he found out about the price he'd have to pay, he decided he didn't want to pay it.

He had the dream, but he lacked the commitment to achieve his dream. And that's fine. I didn't hold it against him. He's a great guy, and there's nothing wrong with having a lot of fun out on the links with your pals.

Do you want to get an advanced degree? Do you want a promotion? Maybe you'd like to quit your job and start your own business, make a couple million dollars, or get married and raise a family. Do you want to own your dream home, free and clear? Lose 50 pounds? Quit smoking? Publish a book?

All goals worth achieving come at a price. You may have to invest money, effort, time, or some other resource. You may have to give up something to get something. Very likely, none of this will be easy, and you'll have to follow through for quite a while—maybe years.

To do what you have to do, you'll need *commitment*. Know what's required of you, then either become dedicated to doing the hard things or choose a different goal. Not everyone is ready or willing to pay the price. It's a personal choice. That's why not everyone's a multi-millionaire.

What is COMMITMENT?

Commitment is a steadfast dedication to a particular cause, goal, relationship, or course of action. It involves a strong sense of obligation to follow through with your intentions or promises despite any challenges or setbacks that may arise.

Why commitment is important:

The truth: almost nothing worthwhile comes easy. By persisting in spite of sacrifices or time invested and with hard work, you can achieve difficult outcomes, whether for yourself or your team. When you've been assigned a project that is key to your organization's success, people will depend on your ability to stay focused and motivated and sustain a high level of effort until you achieve the desired results.

"There's no abiding success without commitment."

Anthony Robbins, American author

What you can do to strengthen your commitment:

- ✓ Start small. Choose a relatively easy first task and follow through.
- ✓ Take action to express commitment and support in your long-term relationships.
- ✓ If you're raising a child, continue to be there with love, support, guidance, and sacrifices.
- ✓ Before committing to a project, check what's involved to ensure that you have the desire to do what's required.
- ✓ Agree to do a difficult task and follow through.
- ✓ Each day, make an effort to go above and beyond your job requirements to help your organization achieve a difficult project.
- ✓ Volunteer for a charitable enterprise and stay committed to contributing your time and energy.
- ✓ Work on developing a new leadership skill until you achieve your goal.

Remember that commitment is a behavior pattern. The more you put it into practice, the stronger it will get. Along the way, you can expect both successes and frustrations. So partner with someone to coach you with encouragement; then learn from your attempts, stick with it, and you'll get stronger over time.

"Desire is the key to motivation, but it's the determination and commitment to an unrelenting pursuit of your goal, a commitment to excellence, that will enable you to attain the success you seek."

Mario Andretti, Italian race car driver

Follow intentions with unrelenting action, and watch dreams become reality.

"Our duty is to be useful, not according to our desires, but according to our powers."

Henri Frédéric Amiel, Swiss philosopher

"Do something every day that you don't want to do; this is the golden rule for acquiring the habit of doing your duty without pain."

Mark Twain, American novelist

"Resolve to perform what you ought. Perform without fail what you resolve."

Benjamin Franklin, American scientist

"In the long run, we shape our lives, and we shape ourselves. The process never ends until we die. And the choices we make are ultimately our responsibility."

Eleanor Roosevelt, American diplomat

26

Responsibility

Do more than what is required, and you will prosper.

The other day, a neighbor and I were talking about the conflicts troubling our property owners association. "You should run for office," he said.

I let that thought sink in. *No. I shouldn't.* I already have a full plate. I've served on association boards before, and if I volunteered for this now, I wouldn't be able to fulfill the responsibilities I already have. But for a moment, I doubted myself. Was I avoiding my community responsibility?

Often, there's a grand, romantic view of "duty"—that it's about completing some heroic or exalted mission. Your duty to serve your country. To help save a life. To save an enterprise from failure. To "give back."

But worthy responsibilities don't have to be lofty undertakings. Some of the most important duties in life are the simple, practical ones right in front of you. Who will fix the fence? Who will move the neighbor's trash can when the wind blows it into the street? Who will clean the mess in the kitchen? Who will replace the burned-out light bulb? It can be hard to see mundane tasks as significant responsibilities. If they're small and uninteresting, it's tempting to think *It's no big deal. Somebody else will take care of it.*

When we lived in Vero Beach, Florida, our home was only a few blocks from the Atlantic Ocean. Walking along the beach after work was a frequent delight. More often than not, these walks turned into trash pick-up projects. Inorganic waste is unsightly and dangerous to pelicans, gulls, and other seabirds. Our arms would be full of debris by the time we found a trash receptacle.

Seemingly trivial acts can make a difference. You take care of them without being asked simply because you know they'll contribute to the general betterment of things. You appreciate the importance of what you've done, even if no one else notices. And your reward is the improvement you see in the world around you and the good feeling you have about yourself because you "took care of business."

In the end, you don't have to be the one to take responsibility for everything, even if you care about it. You choose your tasks. You choose how you'll contribute.

But if the responsibility is a part of your job, then do it. Once you agree to do something, being responsible means that you actually do what you agreed to do. And it means you do it to the best of your abilities. You don't "phone it in." You don't just give it lip service.

In high school, I was captain of the golf team, and I sometimes played two rounds of golf in a day. But my career as an Army officer made it difficult to play often enough to maintain my skills. When my scores steadily declined, golf was no longer fun. So I gave it up, and I haven't played since.

But I still enjoy walking with friends on the golf course. Sometimes, I caddy for them. It's an enjoyable way to get some exercise.

One day, I overheard one of the guys playing in our group say this into his cell phone: "Yeah, I'll take care of it. I'm on my way there right now." I wondered where "there" might be.

"Who was that? You gotta go somewhere?"

"Hey, no way. That was my boss. He thinks I'm in my truck doing deliveries. I love these cell phones," he said as he grinned and walked towards the green.

I was surprised by his willingness to lie so that he could play golf rather than do the job he was being paid to do. Later, I heard that he lost that job and the next one after that.

Adults take responsibility for their children and make most decisions for them. However, children eventually grow into adults, and they then need the inner strength to take responsibility for their own lives and make their own choices.

Of course, it doesn't always work out that way. I've known people who grew up in wealthy families, had everything they wanted given to them, and continued to expect their parents to provide for them well into middle age. I've known people who were raised by parents who protected them from hardship and challenges. As adults, they didn't have the motivation to take responsibility for their own lives. When bad things happened, they blamed other people or external factors for their misfortune.

I've also known people who grew up believing that society or the government was supposed to take care of them.

All these people have a hard time dealing with life. They fail at work. They fail at relationships. And they aren't happy.

What is RESPONSIBILITY?

Responsibility involves accepting and fulfilling the duties and commitments associated with a particular role, position, or relationship. Even when you notice problems that aren't a part of your assigned duties, you take ownership of the need to take effective action. You decide to be the one who will take care of it.

You carry out tasks simply because you know they need to be done.

This sense of responsibility applies to life as much as it does to work. As psychotherapist Nathaniel Branden said: "No one is coming. If I don't do something, nothing is going to get better." You don't wait for someone else to take the initiative. You don't hope they will show up to rescue you from a difficult situation. You do what's necessary.

Why responsibility is important:

Most projects require a team effort, and a lot needs to be done. Much of what happens isn't planned for, and no one has been assigned a role to deal with it. Success depends on people stepping up. When people fail to do this, important things are neglected, and there are failures.

"I am only one, but still I am one. I cannot do everything, but still I can do something. And because I cannot do everything, I will not refuse to do the something that I can do."

Edward Everett Hale, American minister

What you can do to strengthen your responsibility:

- ✓ Maintain a healthy lifestyle.
- ✓ Do the little things to nurture your personal relationships.
- ✓ At work, take the initiative to solve problems, meet deadlines, and collaborate with colleagues.
- ✓ Manage your personal finances by budgeting, paying bills on time, saving for the future, and avoiding excessive debt.

- ✓ Practice eco-friendly habits such as recycling, conserving energy and water, reducing waste, and supporting environmentally sustainable practices.
- ✓ Provide for the well-being of your family, including supporting their physical and emotional needs.
- ✓ Volunteer for community service and charitable causes.

The willingness to take responsibility is a behavior pattern. Putting it into practice can mean extra work, but the more you do it, the easier it gets. Partner with someone who will talk with you about your experiences and give you encouragement. Learn from your attempts to take responsibility, stick with it, and you'll get stronger over time.

"Always do more than is required of you."

George S. Patton, American general

Do what the day requires, and your days will be well spent.

"A strong leader accepts blame and gives the credit."

John Wooden, American college basketball coach

"He that is good for making excuses is seldom good for anything else."

Benjamin Franklin, American scientist

"A person may cause evil to others not only by his actions but by his inaction, and in either case he is justly accountable to them for the injury."

John Stuart Mill, British philosopher

"We are solely responsible for our choices, and we have to accept the consequences of every deed, word, and thought throughout our lifetime."

Elisabeth Kübler-Ross, American author

27

Accountability

Own up to your actions, and you'll stand tall.

The words responsibility and accountability are often used interchangeably. But the two concepts are different. While responsibility is about taking action, accountability is about accepting the consequences of your actions.

Today I opened a new bottle of mouthwash. Like every consumable product with a cap, it had a seal. If you're younger than thirty years old, you probably don't remember a time when products had no seals. The story behind the seals is instructive.

In 1986, someone broke into some bottles of Tylenol and laced them with cyanide. The same kind of malicious product sabotage had happened a few years before, killing seven people. The first time this happened, the Johnson & Johnson company failed to handle the crisis well, and the resulting scare caused their market value to fall by more than a billion dollars. By the second time, the company had learned its lesson. It immediately ordered a recall of its product from every retail outlet. They announced they were responsible for delivering a safe product, and so Tylenol would not be distributed again until they found a way to protect it from this kind of tampering.

As a result, they invented a seal so that someone would have to break the seal to open the container and tamper with its contents. The seals signified positive assurance for the consumer that the product was safe. The solution was so effective that companies everywhere developed similar seals for their products. Now, almost everything is manufactured with a tamper-proof seal.

Johnson and Johnson soon recovered its lost market value and market share, as well as the cost of destroying the product. In fact, they now have the well-earned reputation of being a consumer champion.

Actions have consequences.

Even with good intentions, things don't always go as you expect. Sometimes, you make a mistake or fail to do everything you need to do. Unexpected problems can challenge you. While shortfalls may be embarrassing, the thing to do is to admit to yourself—and others—that *you* were responsible.

And yet, it's hard to say, "It was my fault." You may be concerned that if you admit your mistake, people will think poorly of you. You might have to make amends. The temptation is to let the blame fall somewhere else.

The truth is, people respect a person who stands up and "faces the music." They believe anyone who does so is reliable, will probably deal honestly with them, and can be trusted. They know people make mistakes, and they don't expect you to be perfect. Besides, it's futile to try to sidestep accountability. The truth is almost always discovered.

The question is, will you be seen for your strength or for your weakness?

What is ACCOUNTABILITY?

Accountability means accepting the consequences of your actions. You understand the impact of your choices and acknowledge your behavior, performance, and adherence to commitments, standards, or expectations. You own your responsibilities and are willing to be evaluated on what you have done. When there are failures, you don't let others take the blame. You acknowledge mistakes and take appropriate actions to rectify errors.

Why accountability is important:

People respect individuals who have the inner strength to own up to their mistakes and commit to remedying the consequences. While you may be tempted to blame others, attempts to avoid accountability almost never work. When the facts are revealed, your reluctance to hold yourself accountable is likely to cause people to stop trusting you, which would damage your relationships. It could also delay dealing with the issue and getting back on track.

"Ninety-nine percent of the failures come from people who have the habit of making excuses."

George Washington Carver, American scientist

What you can do to strengthen your accountability:

- ✓ Start small. If you forget to pick up groceries after work, apologize and take immediate steps to rectify the situation.
- ✓ When you make a mistake, readily admit it and seek solutions to rectify the consequences.
- ✓ If you've been entrusted with a significant responsibility and there have been problems, immediately own up to your role in the shortfall and work to remedy the situation.
- ✓ Pay your bills on time and meet your financial obligations.
- ✓ If you're in a leadership role, accept accountability for the performance of your team.

- ✓ Follow the law and adhere to ethical standards, avoiding illegal or dishonorable activities.
- ✓ After assessing your strengths and weaknesses, actively work towards self-improvement.

Accountability isn't about a single instance of owning up to a mistake. It needs to become a behavior pattern. The more you put it into practice, the more consistent the pattern will become. Along the way, you won't always be successful. So partner with someone to coach you with encouragement; then learn from your attempts, stick with it, and you'll get stronger over time.

"In a marriage, an organization, or a culture, only to the extent that people are willing to hold themselves accountable can we have relationships, enterprises, or a world that works."

Nathaniel Branden, American psychotherapist

Pick up the balls you drop, and people will want to play on your team.

"A life spent making mistakes is not only more honorable but more useful than a life spent doing nothing."

George Bernard Shaw, British playwright

"All the beautiful sentiments in the world weigh less than a single lovely action."

James Russell Lowell, American poet

"Let us not be content to wait and see what will happen, but give us the determination to make the right things happen."

Peter Marshall, British clergyman

"Well begun is half done."

Aristotle, Greek philosopher

28

Initiative

Lay a brick, then another, and your castle will rise.

Before my wife and I moved to the Texas Hill Country, we lived in Vero Beach, Florida, a small, quiet Atlantic-side barrier island community far from the big city. We called it "Paradise." It was awfully easy to "be in the moment" there.

Then, in 2004, we suffered a direct hit from Category 2 Hurricane Frances. A couple of weeks later, we were hit again by Category 3 Hurricane Jeanne. All I can say is it's amazing how adverse life can be sometimes. Some of our friends lost their homes. Hotels on the beach were completely destroyed. We were "lucky." We had flooding in our sunroom, and we had to have our roof replaced. We lost nine trees, including a 100-year-old oak tree in our front yard. Oh, and every plant on our property was blown over. The curbside pile of debris in front of our home was seven feet tall and 75 feet long.

Six months later, we had restored our home and property to better-than-before condition. However, the storms had changed us. During the summer of 2005, as we watched Hurricane Katrina ruin New Orleans on TV, we wondered whether a hurricane that strong could hit our community. That was the year of so many hurricanes that they ran out of alphabet names. One of the hurricanes, Wilma, brought us 120 mph winds, equivalent to Category 2 winds. We lived only 6 feet above sea level. A major hurricane could wash our island away. There wouldn't be anything left to rebuild on.

The question was, should we "head for high ground," as a friend of mine suggested? Or should we take a chance and stay in Paradise? We knew that there would be no safe haven. Every place has both its wonders and its potential disasters. Pick your poison. Vero Beach hadn't had a hurricane in 100 years. Maybe there wouldn't be another one. Maybe we wouldn't like living somewhere else.

Moving is an expensive, soul-crunching process. There's a big difference between thinking about moving and actually doing it. If we were to move, the best option for us would be the Texas Hill Country. We had visited there before, and we knew it was beautiful. We'd be near family—a huge benefit. My wife's parents were in their 80s. Her nieces and nephews were growing into adults, getting married, and having kids. In Florida, we would miss most of that.

But we would need to leave right away. We knew people had left Florida because of the hurricanes. With less demand, property values started to decline. The heated-up real estate bubble seemed ready to burst at any time. If that happened, it would be nearly impossible to sell our home.

The day my wife said, "It's time," we put the home up for sale. We interviewed several realtors and picked the most action-oriented one. That evening, she briefed us on a five-day plan. The next day, we started doing everything she told us to do. Before the week was out, we were on a plane to Texas to find out where we wanted to live.

Back home, we got lucky. After about 15 open houses and over 100 walk-throughs, we had a buyer. The offer was 15% less than what we thought the house was worth, but we took it. We returned to the Hill Country to find our new home, and we got lucky again. We found a better home than we thought we'd find in our price range. And we got lucky a third time. We moved before the bubble burst, so our extra equity allowed us to live in a nicer home.

We closed on our sale, packed, drove to Texas, and began a new life in our new home. Our movers delayed bringing our belongings for almost a month, but we made lemonade. We repainted the interior.

In short, it was a difficult decision and a difficult move, but we were glad we acted when we did. We were a part of the family again. Our landscaping finally started looking beautiful. We made lots of new friends.

It can be scary to go where you haven't gone before. You might be disappointed. You might encounter problems. You might fail.

Life's a lot like fishing. To catch fish, you have to go to the lake, cast your line into the water, experiment with different parts of the lake, and keep trying even though most of the time, your line comes up empty. In other words, you have to take action.

Entrepreneur Nolan Bushnell said, "The critical ingredient is getting off your butt and doing something. It's as simple as that. A lot of people have ideas, but few decide to do something about them now. Not tomorrow. Not next week. But today. The true entrepreneur is a doer, not a dreamer."

I've found that certain things in life produce magic. Of course, one is love. Another is action. Especially massive action—coordinating lots of different actions all at once. We know that some of what we do won't work. But we do things anyway because it gets you down the road, and it's the best way to learn what you need to know. And initiative leads to other opportunities, which wouldn't have been discovered if we hadn't been proactive. Thought is essential, but action is where the magic is. In my business, we believe that the better the idea, the more likely other competitors will already be thinking about doing the same thing. The winners are those who get started first and follow through like crazy.

Do it now. Just do it.

What is INITIATIVE?

Initiative means going beyond what's spelled out in a job description. It means doing something that needs to be done, even when you haven't been told to do it. By initiating action, you demonstrate a proactive mindset, resourcefulness, and a sense of ownership. When you recognize a problem or a need, you take the necessary steps to begin addressing it without waiting for instructions.

Why initiative is important:

When you've been given a role or responsibility, it's impossible to have every possible detail spelled out for you. The need for action—even creative action—could present itself unexpectedly; and to contribute to the team mission, others will need you to just handle it. Your team needs you to deal with problems as they arise. If you always wait for instructions, you could miss opportunities to move forward. Problems might fester, and needed improvements might never take place.

"The secret of getting ahead is getting started. The secret of getting started is breaking your complex overwhelming tasks into small manageable tasks, and then starting on the first one."

Mark Twain, American novelist

What you can do to strengthen your initiative:

✓ At work, be on the lookout for an unmet need.

- ✓ When you recognize that something needs to be done, implement a solution, even if it falls outside your assigned responsibilities.
- ✓ Help organize a neighborhood clean-up day. Recruit volunteers and coordinate logistics.
- ✓ Volunteer your time to help organize fundraising events to support a community need.
- ✓ For your own personal development, enroll in relevant courses, attend workshops, or seek out mentors.
- ✓ Implement eco-friendly practices in your daily life, such as recycling, reducing waste, or advocating for conservation policies.
- ✓ Don't hesitate to ask for help when you need it.

The more you practice taking the initiative, the stronger the behavior pattern will become. Along the way, you can discuss your experiences with someone who will encourage you. Talking about your attempts is a great way to learn from them. Stick with it, and you'll get stronger over time.

"It is not what we intend, but what we do, that makes us useful."

Henry Ward Beecher, American author

Run in place, and people will pass you by.

"There is one thing more powerful than all the armies of the world; and that is an idea whose time has come."

Victor Hugo, French novelist

"The gift of fantasy has meant more to me than my talent for absorbing positive knowledge."

Albert Einstein, American physicist

"The mind, once stretched by a new idea, never regains its original dimensions."

Oliver Wendell Holmes, American author

"Good ideas are not adopted automatically. They must be driven into practice with courageous patience."

Eleanor Roosevelt, American diplomat

29

Creativity

Imagine something better, and your ideas will have room to play.

Every explanation and every principle had its beginning in a single person's mind. Things considered common knowledge today were once considered odd, radical, or even dangerous. A new notion can be unsettling. It may seem strange. It may be unproven. It may challenge what people already know. It may ask them to see things in a new way. It may threaten to change their understanding or even their careers, which took years to establish. The natural tendency is to reject a new notion, regardless of its merits.

Creativity was very much on my mind as I walked among the 400 stalls at Market Days in Wimberley, the second-largest outdoor market in Texas. The monthly event on a dedicated 20-acre site is like a massive combo flea market and arts-and-crafts show. It features an unprecedented variety of off-beat, high-quality stuff.

One of the stalls featured beautiful cups and bowls made by Zulu tribe members out of scrap telephone wire. Yes, you may have to read that sentence again because the idea is so outside the box. The quality of artistry is phenomenal.

It all started when a few men decided to wrap their walking sticks in the discarded colored wire. They discovered they could make patterns, and they moved on to cups and bowls. Soon, they were making so much money doing this that they quit their day jobs.

I was wowed by the creativity. About 40 years ago, I used to co-train a course called "Targeted Innovation" at the Center for Creative Leadership. One of the skills we taught was "divergent thinking." In one exercise, we showed participants an ordinary brick and asked them to list other uses for the brick. The trick was to realize that there were different levels of creative thinking:

Level 1—Other uses of a brick as a construction resource

Level 2—Non-construction uses of the brick in its current form

Level 3—Uses of the brick's materials when you change the brick's form

I think the Zulu tribe members were thinking creatively somewhere between Level 2 and Level 3: *What are some non-telephonic uses of the materials in this telephone cable?* The solution they came up with is magical because you can look at that gorgeous cup as long as you want, and you still can't figure out how they did it.

Of course, this kind of creativity is possible for anyone. But it takes extra mental effort to see beyond the obvious "what is" to "what could be." That's why creativity is a character skill. But if the Zulu tribe members can do it, you can do it. I can do it. The proof of this truism is in the very definition of creativity: the novel association of already existing ideas. The idea of a cup already existed. The scrap phone wire already existed. Putting the two together was novel—a creative idea.

Most people associate creativity with the arts. The reality is that creativity is a necessary tool for everything you do in life. Also, the notion that only gifted people can be creative is nonsense. Anyone can be creative. Coming up with a new way to do something is simply one of the things any normal human brain can do.

Try this exercise: Hold the familiar image of rock star Taylor Swift in your mind. Now, instead of a sparkling, sexy outfit, imagine that she's wearing dirty camouflage fatigues. And instead of holding a microphone, she's holding a multi-colored beach ball. Got this image in your mind? Good.

Well, this scene has never happened before. Even so, you created it in your mind. It's what any normal brain can do.

Now, not all creative combinations turn out to be useful, of course. In fact, most don't. After the lightbulb is turned on, the idea needs to be subjected to analysis or experimentation—to be improved or rejected.

I've been a manager for over 50 years. During this time, I've had to face a lot of problems. Some of these would more aptly be called disasters. But in every single case, what we did to recover and move on in a new way turned out to be superior to the path we were on before things went south. 100% of the time, *we ended up in better shape than if the problems had never happened.*

Once my rice bowl has been shattered, I have to come up with a solution. A replacement rice bowl. Or something else. Something better.

It helps to approach problem-solving with an open mind and to be willing to imagine other ways of doing things. One classic technique is called "brainstorming," which is nothing more than setting aside fifteen or twenty minutes to generate ideas when criticism or judgments aren't allowed. State the problem, then write down as many ideas as you can, regardless of their practical merit. You can evaluate them later.

It also helps to consider lots of ideas because the first creative thoughts you have are rarely the most useful ones.

If you believe in an idea, be ready to champion it. As creativity expert E. Paul Torrance once said, "It takes courage to be creative. Just as soon as you have an idea, you're in a minority of one." Admiral Rickover advised, "Good ideas are not adopted automatically. They must be driven into practice with courageous patience."

Remember that when someone offers you a suggestion. Giving a new idea a fair hearing is a no-lose proposition. Maybe the idea has merit, and you can improve it. If it turns out to be impractical, you can just move on. In the end, the best ideas prove themselves. If knowledge is power, imagination, and open-mindedness give you a significant advantage.

What is CREATIVITY?

Creativity is the ability to generate valuable new ideas, concepts, or solutions through a process of imaginative thinking. It involves combining existing knowledge, experiences, and perspectives in innovative ways to produce something new or unique. Creativity manifests in various forms, such as artistic expression, problem-solving, and invention. By embracing experimentation and evaluating possible solutions, you can break free from approaches that aren't working well anymore.

Why creativity is important:

The reality is that the world is constantly changing. People's needs are changing. To meet these needs and continue to be successful, you—and the people around you—need to be willing to consider fresh ideas. If you continue with conventional ideas, you might struggle to adapt to changing conditions. If you don't think outside the box, you could miss opportunities to contribute new, more effective solutions.

"What is now proved was once only imagined."

William Blake, British poet

What you can do to strengthen your creativity:

- ✓ When faced with an issue, ask yourself: *Is this a simple malfunction that requires troubleshooting and fixing? Or does it make sense to consider a whole new approach?*
- ✓ When what you're doing isn't getting the results you want, try an unconventional method that will push the boundaries of a traditional norm.
- ✓ When faced with an unfamiliar challenge, approach it from a fresh perspective. Ask yourself: *Is there a new solution that will improve efficiency or solve a complex problem*?
- ✓ To stimulate a new insight, challenge an existing assumption.
- ✓ Explore how other areas of work and life solve similar problems. Try to adapt their approaches to what you're doing.
- ✓ When what you're doing isn't working well anymore, try brainstorming. Reach for unconventional ideas by blending solutions from completely different areas.
- ✓ Play with some "What if..." ideas until you have a list of possibilities.

Remember that thinking creatively is a behavior pattern. The more often you search for new ideas, the easier the effort will get. Meet regularly with a like-minded person who can listen to your accounts of your creative efforts and offer encouragement. Continue to learn from your attempts, stick with it, and you'll get stronger over time.

"You see things and you say, 'Why?' But I dream things that never were and I say, 'Why not?'"

George Bernard Shaw, British playwright

Step outside the box and behold 99.9% of what's possible.

"The most important thing you can do to achieve your goals is to make sure that as soon as you set them, you immediately begin to create momentum."

Anthony Robbins, American author

"Never leave till tomorrow that which you can do today."

Benjamin Franklin, American scientist

"Life can only be understood backwards; but it must be lived forwards."

Soren Kierkegaard, Danish philosopher

"Plans are only good intentions unless they immediately degenerate into hard work."

Peter Drucker, American author

30

Proactivity

Court the future you desire, or it will turn its attention to someone else.

When people ask me why I don't do consulting work anymore, I recall the most challenging consulting assignment I ever had, which was to present training in creative problem-solving to the mid-level managers of Banamex (National Bank of Mexico) 40 years ago. It was a memorable experience. During the month I was there, I learned a lot about Mexico, its people, and the language.

But two things made the work particularly difficult.

First, every aspect of the training had to be in Spanish. That meant I had to present through an interpreter, and all my materials—including my brain-based personality assessment—had to be translated into Spanish. What a task that was! I must have been more optimistic and adventurous back then because if I had to do it over, I would have suggested they find someone else.

But I eventually put it all together and shipped it to Juan, the bank's human resources point of contact.

The other thing that made my experience so challenging was Juan. Juan was a great guy. He spoke fluent English, and he treated me with enormous kindness. He made sure I was comfortable and showed me around Mexico City. A family man, he invited me to spend the weekend at his home in Guadalajara. We became friends.

What made Juan a problem was his inability to plan. He was spontaneous about everything. I watched in horror when we arrived at the first hotel and saw that he hadn't reserved any presentation rooms. We had to take what was left. The rooms were too small, and the participants complained. Also, he failed to arrange for the earphone system for the interpreter. I asked him about the activities agenda, and he had none. He said he thought it would be great if the entire group went to a local theater that evening. But he made no reservations, and he didn't make the call for the buses until the participants were standing outside the hotel. We arrived at the theater late. I was appalled, but he seemed happy with everything. I was diplomatic as I pleaded with him to make advance arrangements in the future. He never did, though, program after program, hotel after hotel.

It wasn't a matter of forgetfulness. He seemed unwilling or unable to make the effort to be proactive.

Proactivity requires a kind of mental time travel. You begin in the present, where you sense a problem or a gap between what you want and what you have. Then you visit the future, where you imagine what's possible. Back in the present again, you wonder what you could do to make that future happen, which sends you into the past, where you recall instances of cause and effect that have worked for similar challenges. In the present again, you use those lessons to construct a step-by-step plan to create your desired future. Then, you begin creating the future.

Whew! No wonder Juan disliked proactivity! That's why it's considered a character skill—because it takes real effort to translate a vision into action.

Desire is good, but to get what you want, you have to go beyond that. As the saying goes: "Good days don't just happen. You make them happen."

If you want your kids to go to college, you know it's going to be even more expensive when they're ready than it is today. Maybe they'll get scholarships, student loans, and part-time jobs. But if their education really means that much to you when they're small, you'll set up a system to save the money.

If you don't like being blown away by a crisis, look to the future to see problems building. It's a lot easier to solve problems while they're still small. If you want to avoid a fatal heart attack, change your exercise and eating habits now, not after the first signs of heart disease.

What is PROACTIVITY?

Proactivity involves envisioning what could happen in the future. It means acting in anticipation of future circumstances rather than waiting to react to them. Put another way, you act before there is an immediate need in order to prevent a problem from ever coming up. Using a forward-thinking mindset, you focus on identifying opportunities, planning, and taking steps to achieve desired future outcomes or prevent potential problems.

Why proactivity is important:

Proactivity gives you more control over what can happen to you. If you don't reach for solutions before the need arises, you might be surprised by an issue, or an opportunity could pass you by. It's nearly impossible to create change without being proactive. Inaction and complacency can lead to a lack of progress or even failure.

"I skate where the puck is going to be, not where it has been."

Wayne Gretzky, Canadian ice hockey player

What you can do to strengthen your proactivity:

- ✓ The next time you set a goal, anticipate possible roadblocks, arrange for resources, and track progress along the way.
- ✓ Create a schedule to ensure you meet deadlines.
- ✓ Even if things seem to be running smoothly, evaluate one of your current routines to discover a better way.
- ✓ Examine your work to discover a possible future issue, then talk with your team about dealing with it before it escalates.
- ✓ For your own health, engage in regular exercise, maintain a balanced diet, and seek preventive healthcare, such as getting regular check-ups or vaccinations.
- ✓ Initiate open and honest communication among coworkers to address concerns, foster understanding, and prevent conflicts.
- ✓ Look at how you work and ask yourself: *What unexpected things could happen if I continue doing this?*
- ✓ Ask your team: *What needs to be done right now that's not getting done?*

It takes a forward-seeing perspective to initiate proactivity. This skill is a behavior pattern. The more you practice being proactive, the more natural it will come to you. Along the way, you may fail to be proactive and suffer the consequences. Ask someone to discuss your successful and not-so-successful experiences with you and give encouragement. As you learn from your attempts, stick with it, and you'll get stronger over time.

"If one advances confidently in the direction of his dreams, and endeavors to live the life which he has imagined, he will meet with a success unexpected in common hours."

Henry David Thoreau, American philosopher

Repair the roof on a sunny day, and you won't have to do it when it's leaking.

"Nothing would be done at all if one waited until one could do it so well that no one could find fault with it."

John Henry Newman, British clergyman

"Indecision is the thief of opportunity."

Jim Rohn, American author

"Nothing is more difficult, and therefore more precious, than to be able to decide."

Napoleon Bonaparte, French emperor

"I am not a product of my circumstances. I am a product of my decisions."

Stephen Covey, American author

31

Decisiveness

Know when to stop thinking and when to start doing.

"You're about to make a career-changing decision." Have you ever heard that warning?

I earned my Ph.D. in English midway through my career as an Army officer. I was a captain about to be promoted to major. But I considered walking away from that career to start a new one as an English professor. It was a momentous decision. A whole new career teaching literature seemed exciting. I love literature and had established myself as an authority on the contemporary American novel. There were job openings. I could pay my dues, and my work ethic would help me move up.

On the other hand, I knew about university politics. If anything, they were nastier than politics in the military. Also, in the beginning, I'd have to teach a lot of mandatory basic writing courses to kids who didn't want to be there. In order to advance, I'd have to publish—or perish. And I knew what kind of esoteric nonsense got published.

Also, I'd have to give up my pension. Of course, that would be replaced by another pension. But I knew that this was the time to decide because each year going forward, I'd have more time invested in my military career, and it would be harder to give it up. The two paths led to radically different futures.

In the end, I chose to remain in the Army. Why? Because along the way, I had discovered a fascination for the topic of leadership. Working in this area was a way to make a difference. I imagined my future as an expert in leadership, teaching managers how to get the best effort from their people. Teaching an appreciation of poetry and fiction didn't have the same kind of impact, not by a long shot.

Also, I had to admit that every assignment I had in the Army had enriched me so far. I felt sure I could keep this going for ten more years. Surely, I could get assignments that would continue to build on my experience and knowledge of leadership. I had to admit that my love of literature was satisfied by reading it, not by writing about it or teaching it.

I never regretted the decision. My assignments during the second half of my career included director of human resources for an organization with 20,000 employees, program manager for developing doctrine for Army training, director of personnel management for the Armed Forces Staff College, and teaching leadership as head of the ROTC program at the College of William and Mary. These assignments were interesting and a fantastic preparation for the consulting business I started after I retired.

Not every decision lends itself to such thorough analysis. Sometimes the advantages and disadvantages—the benefits and costs—aren't so clear. And sometimes, you don't have much time to do this analysis.

Several years before my company became a product company, I spent most of my time speaking and consulting. And, of course, I had to market my services, which was an ongoing necessity and challenge for someone new to the business.

One day, I got a call from a friend who was working at a large consulting firm. "An association of retired CEOs is chartering a cruise ship," he said. "They plan to travel around the Caribbean for ten days, combining fun and education. They want us to do an on-board program, but they don't want to pay us for it. My company is passing. Do you want the gig? You'll only have to present for an hour. Other than that, you can enjoy the cruise. You can bring your wife. They're going to some cool places and meeting with Castro and other big-deal personalities in the region. And you'll be rubbing shoulders with some well-connected business leaders who might bring you some business."

I didn't know whether to get involved. My consulting practice was relatively new, and the prospect of finding new clients was tempting. On the other hand, these were retired CEOs. And I didn't like the idea of being out of pocket for two weeks. That seemed like a high price to pay for prospecting. The cost was clear, but the benefits were not. So I wasn't sure what to do.

But something inside me told me to go for it. "Count me in," I said.

Well, it was a memorable cruise, and they liked my program. I met quite a few successful business people. One of them was Bob Midlothian, a retired CEO who lived in Miami Beach and who later became a friend and mentor. Over the years, we helped each other on several projects.

On one occasion, Bob asked me to coach a banker he was working with. On my next business trip to Miami, I met with her, and the session went well. She was so delighted that she insisted on giving me a Saturday tour of her favorite Miami venues. We became friends and corresponded from time to time.

Several years later, my marriage ended. My friendship with my banker friend evolved, and eventually, we got married. So, my decision to work for free turned out to be a momentous one. If I had turned down this pro bono project, I would have missed the cruise, I never would have met Bob, and he would have never introduced me to my wife.

How could I have known that my decision would have enormous personal consequences? Decisions sometimes work this way. The consequences are not always predictable or momentous. Forks in the road of life aren't always well-marked, so you have to look out over the horizon to sense what's coming. Any path can lead to something significant, so it pays to listen to your intuition.

Decisiveness boils down to two things:

1. Using the available time to identify the possible courses of action, get input, research the related factors, and compare your options.
2. Commit to a decision at the moment of greatest opportunity—and act.

Much of what you'd like to know may be impossible to learn, especially future consequences. And the door of opportunity may start closing before you have time to fully study your options. But often, you should move forward anyway, relying on your ability to learn as you go and your flexibility to change course if necessary.

Nobody said being decisive was easy. That's why it's considered a character skill.

What is DECISIVENESS?

Effective decision-making depends on timing—judging how much time you have before you must act. Ideally, before you act on a situation, you evaluate the pros and cons first. If you have time to do so, you consider potential issues, opportunities, needed resources, and consequences, then move forward in a prompt, resolute manner—not too soon and not too late. If there's no time for this kind of analysis, you take prompt action based on whatever input you already have.

Why decisiveness is important:

The road to success is built with good decisions. Faulty decisions can create horrible consequences. With your mind already made up and in a rush to move forward, you might fail to consider important factors or other ideas. On the other hand, you don't want to overthink a problem. If you study a situation too long, it may be too late to act effectively. Decisiveness depends on assessing accurately the window of opportunity. *Timing is everything.*

"If we wait for the moment when everything, absolutely everything is ready, we shall never begin."

Ivan Turgenev, Russian novelist

What you can do to strengthen your decisiveness:

- ✓ The next time you face a crisis, first evaluate whether you need to act quickly to coordinate solutions and resources to prevent harm or damage.
- ✓ If you should face a critical project delay, promptly analyze the causes and the roadblocks, then reallocate resources to get the project back on track.
- ✓ If you realize that a toxic relationship has been causing you harm, consider ending the relationship.
- ✓ When faced with the need to decide and act, first ask yourself: *What is the ideal timeframe to move ahead with a solution?*
- ✓ When struggling with an issue, ask yourself if you're reaching for perfection when a "really good" solution would suffice.

Judging how much thought you can afford to invest before you need to move forward is a behavior pattern. The more you exercise effective decision-making, the more adept and confident you'll become at making these judgments. Along the way, you may experience both successes and shortfalls. It's a good idea to partner with someone you can have regular discussions with about how you're making decisions. It will help you learn from your attempts and get the kind of encouragement that will help you stick with it as you get stronger over time.

"To reach a port we must sail, sometimes with the wind and sometimes against it. But we must not drift or lie at anchor."

Oliver Wendell Holmes, American author

While there's still time, check and reflect—and you'll decide with confidence.

"When you reach the end of your rope, tie a knot on it and hang on."

Thomas Jefferson, American president

"For the resolute and determined there is time and opportunity."

Ralph Waldo Emerson, American philosopher

"Most of the things worth doing in the world had been declared impossible before they were done."

Louis Brandeis, American jurist

"The difference between the impossible and the possible lies in an individual's determination."

Tommy Lasorda, American professional baseball manager

32

Perseverance

If you never give up, it will be very hard to beat you.

I'm a sports fan. I love the thrill of victory and the agony of defeat. Thanks to television, I've witnessed some of the greatest moments in the history of sports. As I think back, the most exciting moments happened because athletes who were about to lose in major competitions refused to give up.

My first memory of such an athlete was Sugar Ray Leonard, who fought Thomas Hearns for the "unified" Welterweight Championship in "The Showdown" at Caesar's Palace in 1981. Hearns was a powerful, aggressive puncher (32-0, 30 KO), and Leonard was a fast, stylish boxer (30-1, 22 KO). Hearns pounded Leonard during the first five rounds. I remember one blow that brought Leonard to his knees. The image shocked me. One of his eyes was nearly swollen shut, and I could see the shock and pain on his face. But he got up and kept going. Leonard fought with new energy in the next three rounds, but then Hearns regrouped to dominate Leonard and take a commanding lead in the 12th round. Leonard's trainer, the legendary Angelo Dundee, shouted at him, "You're blowing it!"

Leonard fought furiously in the 13th round, knocking Hearns down twice. The fight was stopped in the 14th. Leonard won by technical knockout.

So, for me, the word "perseverance" often invokes the image of Sugar Ray Leonard in pain, refusing to give up. Life delivers its heavy blows, which can bring us to our knees. We can either quit or get up and keep on fighting. If we refuse to give up, we still have a chance to win.

One of the great rivalries in sports is the New York Yankees and the Boston Red Sox. The Yankees have been loved and loathed for winning so often—especially the World Series. The Red Sox were known, until 2004, as the team that couldn't get it done in the World Series. And that's what was happening in the 2004 American League Championship Series. The Yankees had won the first three games and were ahead in the last inning of the decisive fourth game. But the Red Sox were able to score and tie the game. Curt Schilling's sock was soaked in blood as he pitched with a ruptured ankle tendon. The Red Sox hung on until the 12th inning, when a home run gave them the victory. Then they did what had never been done before in the history of baseball: they won the seven-game series after being down 0-3. Later, they swept the St. Louis Cardinals in four games to win the World Series.

Another favorite example of perseverance was the 1980 Wimbledon title match between John McEnroe and Bjorn Borg, often cited as the best Wimbledon final ever played. McEnroe started strong, winning the first set. But Borg won the next two sets and was about to win the third, decisive set. He had McEnroe down 5-4, but McEnroe saved 5 match points to make it 5-5. Then Borg survived 6 set points. McEnroe eventually won the set to even the match at two sets each. It was a huge setback for Borg. Only one point from victory, now the match was even. McEnroe had stolen the momentum and, in the first game of the final set, was about to break Borg's serve, 15-40. Just when McEnroe seemed to be cruising to victory, Borg dug deep and reeled off 19 straight points to win the set and the match, his fifth consecutive Wimbledon victory.

And then there was Michael Jordan in the 1997 NBA Finals. The series was tied 2-2, and in game 5, Jordan was seriously ill. His doctors said he had food poisoning or a stomach virus. Coach Phil Jackson said, "Standing up was nauseating for him and caused dizzy spells." League MVP Karl Malone and John Stockton had Utah up by 16 points in the second quarter, but through the force of his will, Jordan slowly got the Bulls back in the game. Later, he said, "In the third quarter, I felt like I couldn't catch my wind and get my energy level up. I don't know how I got through the fourth quarter. I was just trying to gut myself through it." He inspired his teammates, and the game was tied with less than a minute to go. Jordan scored, and the Bulls edged the Jazz 90-88. As sick as he was, the 34-year-old Jordan played 44 of 48 minutes, scoring 38 points. Unable to walk, his teammates carried him back to the locker room. The Bulls won the next game to take the championship.

And that reminds me of another great basketball story, the 1983 college men's championship, which was won by the North Carolina State Wolfpack, coached by Jim Valvano. At the end of the regular season, NC State was 17-10 and wouldn't have been selected for the tournament, but somehow they won the ACC Tournament, which qualified them for an automatic slot. During their tournament streak, they won by close margins against top-ranked teams like North Carolina (Michael Jordan and James Worthy), Virginia (Ralph Sampson), and Houston (Hakeem Olajuwon). The final play against Houston was a desperation airball from 30 feet, which was caught and dunked in the final second to give State the 54-52 victory.

The classic "Cinderella" team, NC State shouldn't have gone far in the tournament, but they played their hearts out every minute, and they refused to give up.

People sometimes make fun of me for telling sports stories to illustrate character skills. But I don't care. I find them inspiring. And we certainly need the inspiration. Life can sometimes challenge us to our limits.

Twenty-seven years ago, my wife had breast cancer. The surgeon removed a small Stage 1 lump, but the fear was that the cancer could come back. Someday, a small cancer still left somewhere in her body might grow into a large one. To attack cancer cells that might still be in other parts of the body, the doctors recommended a regimen of radiation and chemotherapy.

Of course, the therapy was optional. In her heart, my wife wasn't sure she could endure it. She called her sister, who said, "You've got to do it."

"But I don't think I have the strength to do this for eight months."

Her sister's reply: "You don't have to. Each day, you only have to have enough strength for that day."

So, my wife endured her treatment one day at a time. It was tough on her. The poison disabled her physically and mentally. At one point, her white blood count got so low she had to take special shots every day. Afterward, it took more than two years for her to recover from the treatment. She's been cancer-free ever since.

What is PERSEVERANCE?

Perseverance means remaining steadfast in the face of challenges, obstacles, or setbacks. It's the ability to maintain commitment and effort over an extended period while overcoming difficulties. Very little that is worthwhile comes easy. Faced with adversity, you resist the temptation to give up. You gather your patience, willpower, and a positive attitude to keep moving forward and continue making progress.

Why perseverance is important:

The problem with quitting is that if you do, you're done. Whatever goal or benefit you were aspiring to is now beyond your reach. Quitting has a horrible impact on self-esteem. And it can become a habit, forever limiting what you can achieve for yourself. Organizations need leaders and team members who willingly do the hard things. They need and value people who have the strength to persevere regardless of any adversity they may face.

"It's hard to beat a person who never gives up."

Babe Ruth, American professional baseball player

What you can do to strengthen your perseverance:

- ✓ When working through an unforeseen challenge, don't quit until you have resolved it.
- ✓ Rededicate yourself to finishing a difficult project. Persist in spite of mistakes, difficulties, changes, or lack of support.
- ✓ Practice and refine a skill, then stay with it until you reach a level of mastery.
- ✓ People everywhere experience injury, trauma, tragedy, or loss. If this happens to you, pick yourself up and persist until you fully recover your well-being.
- ✓ When advocating for social change or justice, persist in your efforts to raise awareness, mobilize others, and create change.
- ✓ Take up a hobby that has piqued your interest. Resolve that you won't quit just because the required skills are hard to learn.
- ✓ If you find yourself facing financial difficulty, get advice to create a plan, and don't abandon your effort until you're in good shape again.

By repeatedly exercising perseverance in tough situations, you can become a consistent champion. While the road to building this strength may involve both successes and disappointments, you can partner with someone to coach you with encouragement; then learn from your attempts, stick with it, and you'll get stronger over time.

"Great works are performed not by strength, but by perseverance."

Samuel Johnson, British essayist

Refuse to quit, and you'll go further than you thought possible.

"Always make a total effort, even when the odds are against you."

Arnold Palmer, American professional golfer

"I can't imagine a person becoming a success who doesn't give his game of life everything he's got."

Walter Cronkite, American journalist

"The first requisite for success is the ability to apply your physical and mental energies to one problem incessantly without growing weary."

Thomas Edison, American inventor

"The highest compliment that you can pay me is to say that I work hard every day."

Wayne Gretzky, Canadian ice hockey player

33

Effort

Outwork people with more talent, and you will finish first.

Is your birthday a big deal to you?

I'm the kind of guy who doesn't like to celebrate his birthday. I like to say, "If you want to give me a present, for heaven's sake don't wait until my birthday." I also say, "On my birthday I'll be one day older than the day before." I like the idea that every single day of my life is the most special day, not just the one day marking my birth all those years ago.

My wife, on the other hand, loves celebrating her birthday. To her, it's a supremely important day, and she reminds me several times well in advance to make sure I don't forget. And I never do. I think of it as one more way I can bring some happiness into her life—one of my highest priorities.

Sometimes, though, pulling off a successful birthday for her isn't so easy. To make sure I hit the bulls-eye, I always ask, "Honey, what would you like for your birthday this year?" Simple, huh?

Not always. Several years ago, I asked the magic question. We had just moved from Florida to the Texas Hill Country, and we were busy transforming a house into a home. And so her reply was, "I miss the ocean. I miss the water. I want a waterfall in the backyard."

Uh-oh. Waterfalls can be expensive. When I asked her to be more specific, she said we could pick out a nice one at Lowes, The Home Depot, or a store specializing in water features. I'd never seen a ready-made one that wasn't tacky, and paying to have one built could run five figures—or more. This was beginning to sound like a major request.

The bottom line: I decided to build the waterfall myself. I had never built a water feature before, but once I built—all by myself—a two-level, 500-square-foot backyard deck with built-in seats, which turned out great. If I could do that, I felt confident I could build a waterfall. Besides, our home was situated on a limestone ridge, and rocks of all sizes were all over our property. I'd dig a big hole in the chosen spot, then move a bunch of rocks from where I didn't want them to where I did want them.

To make a long story short, the waterfall turned out great. But not without a major effort on my part. I ended up moving over two tons of rocks—by hand. On the plus side, I didn't have to work out at the gym during that period. On the negative side, one of the rocks weighed 400 pounds. I used a handcart, but do you have any idea how hard it is to maneuver a rock that size onto a cart? I tried and failed over 20 times before I finally got it onto the cart. It took me four hours to figure it out. I just kept trying until something worked. Then, I had to haul it up the hill. I thought the cart would break.

Then, there was the plumbing, which turned out to be a much more delicate task than I envisioned. The pipes come from the pump inside the hole to around the side of the waterfall, then up the backside, and split into two openings. All these unsightly white pipes have to be covered with lovely rocks. I had to redo the pipes three times before I got it right.

And there were the leaks. Well, you get the idea. It was a lot of work. In retrospect, I have to say it was the most difficult project I've ever attempted.

It took me two months of unrelenting effort (and $500 worth of materials) to finish it, but the result was worth it. It looked natural, and the landscaping grew up around it. It attracted frogs and birds. At night in the spring and fall, we could hear the sound of falling water from our open bedroom window. Best of all, my wife said it was the best birthday present she's ever had.

During my life, I've learned that sometimes, I need to do some really hard work to get what I want. The price in effort may be substantial, but it almost always pays off. Like the time over 40 years ago, when I had to submit my dissertation by a specific date. I was living in Germany at the time, so I had to finish the writing, proof it, revise it, copy it, and send it in time for my committee to review before the deadline. My wife and I planned a vacation to the Canary Islands as a reward. It took a lot of hard work, and it meant back-to-back all-nighters before hauling the copies to the post office. We were so tired that we slept for the first two days of that vacation. But a few months later I was at Duke University shaking hands with the members of my committee, and they were calling me Dr. Coates. Special moments like this can make you believe in hard work.

If you're like me, you know that what you want most will not be given to you. You won't win the lottery, and you won't have a rich uncle who'll pass on a big inheritance.

No, what's really going to happen is that you're going to choose which race you want to run. Then you'll pay the price. You'll commit yourself to the kind of total effort that will give you a chance to win. You'll concentrate all your energies on the challenge, and you'll give the best you have to offer.

What is EFFORT?

You bring effort to your work by exerting significant physical and mental energy to accomplish a task, goal, or objective. It means consistently doing your best, applying your abilities and determination to achieve a desired outcome, even if it means a lot of hard work and deferring more pleasant activities. If the work involves skills you don't have, you invest time and effort to acquire them.

Why effort is important:

When you're working towards a worthy goal, much of what has to be done won't be easy. Leaders need people who will work hard to achieve high-quality results. The people who work with you will need you to pitch in. Of course, it would be easier to just meet minimum expectations or let other people do most of the work. But if you stay focused and dedicated as you push through obstacles and make progress, the hard aspects of work will get done. Your team will succeed, and you'll gain the respect of the people around you.

"Be the hardest working person you can be. That's how you separate yourself from the competition."

Stephen Curry, American professional basketball player

What you can do to strengthen the level of your effort:

- ✓ Choose a project that interests you, then give it your best effort until you achieve it.
- ✓ When working on a tough assignment, break tasks into manageable steps and persistently do what's necessary until you finish it.
- ✓ Invest your creativity to find a solution to a complex problem.
- ✓ When faced with an obstacle, work through it until you resolve it.
- ✓ When needed, show up early and stay late to get the job done.

- ✓ Take on additional responsibilities, pursue professional development opportunities, and actively seek to enhance your skills and knowledge.
- ✓ Follow a physical workout routine, pushing yourself to increase endurance, strength, or flexibility gradually.
- ✓ Volunteer time and effort to support charitable organizations.
- ✓ Make the effort to improve a sports skill; practice until you are proficient.
- ✓ Sign up for a college course and work hard on it until you get an A.

Your goal is to make a habit of working hard to give your best effort. The more you do this, the more it will become your go-to response to any task or project. As you grow stronger, it will help if you partner with someone who cares about your success to help you learn from your attempts and encourage you to stick with it.

"I'm a great believer in luck, and I find the harder I work the more I have of it."

Thomas Jefferson, American president

Invest great effort, and you'll earn great dividends.

"Perfection is not attainable, but if we chase perfection we can catch excellence."

Vince Lombardi, American professional football coach

"We aim above the mark to hit the mark."

Ralph Waldo Emerson, American philosopher

"High expectations are the key to everything."

Sam Walton, American business leader

"The richest reward of all is being proud of your work."

Jan Carlzon, Swedish business leader

34

Excellence

Do your best work, and people will want you to do it again and again.

Often, when I watch a movie, I do so alone because my wife would much rather read a mystery novel. So when she said she wanted to see the new Sherlock Holmes movie, I quickly agreed.

But I had reservations. I had seen the previews, and I understood that this was not going to be the traditional Sherlock Holmes. His character had been remade into some kind of action hero. We went anyway, of course, and I was delighted with two things.

First, Robert Downey, Jr. delivered an amazing acting performance. His challenge was to create an all-new image of Sherlock Holmes that would appeal to young 21st-century viewers while preserving and perhaps even deepening the character's traditional essence. And he pulled it off—with a British accent! I can't imagine how difficult that must have been. Only two or three other actors could have done as well. That level of effort and that much attention to detail is impressive.

I noticed the same level of achievement in the production. The sets and costumes made 19th-century London seem absolutely real. Infinite pains were taken with so many details. Once again, the level of quality was impressive.

I love it when artists achieve a very high level of excellence when they attempt a high level of difficulty and pull it off. I don't like B-grade art. It's not impressive or enjoyable when I conclude that practically anyone could have done as well.

I was involved in my own quest for excellence while in graduate school at Duke University. I decided to write my dissertation on John Cheever, an American novelist who, in his lifetime, was considered America's finest storyteller. Very little criticism had been written about him, so to write a meaningful dissertation I would need to know more about him. The author agreed to an interview, and we became friends. I moved to West Point to teach English, so it was easy to visit him once a month at his home in Ossining, New York. During our talks, he revealed far more to me than I could use in my dissertation.

One day, he came down the stairs with a manuscript in his hand. "I have written a story," he said. This surprised me because he was nearing the end of his career and hadn't published a story in quite a while. "Would you like to hear it?"

We sat at his dining room table while he put his hand on mine and read the story. It was "The Leaves, The Lion-fish and the Bear," which was published in *Esquire* in 1974. It was a wonderful story, and I was the first person to enjoy it. What a gift!

Afterward, John wanted to go for a walk. It was a cold, blustery day, and when we reached the top of the hill above his property, he said, "I'm freezing. Will you hold me?" Cheever was like a surrogate father to me, so I quickly agreed. But I soon discovered that he also wanted sex. I dealt with that uncomfortable situation as tactfully as I could, and we returned to his house. But my mind was connecting the dots. I now realized that his bisexuality was evident in most of his fiction, and I hadn't noticed it. When I pointed this out, he agreed and said it would be fine with him if I treated this theme in my dissertation.

To do the topic justice, I decided to rewrite my entire dissertation. And something else—in the rewriting, I would discard the academic tone and adopt a more straightforward storytelling style. The story was important, and I wanted people to know about it.

It was hard to rewrite my dissertation, but my decision to reach for excellence paid off. My committee thought it was the most readable dissertation they had ever seen, and I got my Ph.D. More significantly, the facts surrounding Cheever's sexual orientation became more widely known. After he died in 1982, all three of his biographers treated his sexuality as the central theme of his life, and they described my encounter with him as the catalyst for his "coming out of the closet." My comprehensive bibliography was published and remains a standard reference for Cheever scholars to this day. So, I became a minor footnote to literary history, which is a more satisfying result than what usually issues from dissertations.

But excellence makes a difference in ordinary life, too. I recall that in those days I often felt overwhelmed by my work. I'd come home to my family exhausted, and sometimes, when my sons wanted me to read a story, I'd go through the motions just to get through it. And when friends gathered, I half-stepped my way through conversations. I had a full plate, and sometimes, I superficially handled other obligations.

So when I remember what my life was like then, I feel a mixture of pride and regret. From the perspective of decades of experience, I wish I had taken more pains to do even the small, everyday things so well that something wonderful happened—even when I was tired. It was a hard lesson to learn, and the lesson was about *excellence*.

What is EXCELLENCE?

Excellence is about achieving very high-quality results. Good enough is never good enough. You consistently push beyond the boundaries of what is considered ordinary or average. High standards of performance, achievement, or conduct—that surpass expectations—drive you.

Why excellence is important:

In any endeavor, results can range from poor to outstanding. Some people don't value excellence. For them, meeting minimum standards is good enough. They aren't motivated to give the extra effort needed to achieve high quality. These individuals hold the team back, making it hard to achieve difficult goals. When people value and understand high quality and if they try to achieve it, they can attain any goal a team sets for itself.

"The power of excellence is overwhelming. It is always in demand and nobody cares about its color."

Daniel James, American general

What you can do to strengthen your ability to achieve excellence:

- ✓ At work, make an effort to consistently exceed expectations.
- ✓ Study high quality wherever you find it; learn what it looks like—what's possible.
- ✓ Inspire and empower others to achieve outstanding results.
- ✓ If your role involves interacting with customers, consistently provide exceptional service by exceeding their expectations and resolving issues promptly and effectively.
- ✓ If you participate in sports, practice skills until you can consistently perform at a high level.

- ✓ The next time you do a chore—it could be a routine task, such as mowing the lawn—make an effort to take the finished result to a new level.
- ✓ By doing the little things exceedingly well, you establish a reputation for excellence.

Your efforts should be to make excellence a habit. The more you reach for the highest levels of quality, the stronger the behavior pattern will get. Along the way, you might be disappointed in one of your efforts. Having a like-minded person to help you learn from your attempts and encourage you will help you stick with it as you get stronger over time.

"If a man can write a better book, preach a better sermon, or make a better mousetrap than his neighbor, though he build his house in the woods, the world will make a beaten path to his door."

Ralph Waldo Emerson, American philosopher

Do ordinary things in an extraordinary way, and people will wonder how you did it.

"The peace I am thinking of is the dance of an open mind when it engages another equally open one."

Toni Morrison, American novelist

"It is never too late to give up our prejudices."

Henry David Thoreau, American philosopher

"It is not who is right, but what is right, that is important."

Thomas H. Huxley, British biologist

"No sensible man ever imputes inconsistency to another for changing his mind."

Marcus Tullius Cicero, Roman orator

35

Open-mindedness

Open your mind, and new knowledge will come rushing in.

In many high-rise buildings, certain floors have a single tenant or facility, and the elevators that serve these floors have special security keys that limit access. No one can visit that part of the building without this special key.

People who are unwilling to consider new information are like that. They control the intellectual key that keeps nonresident information out.

Thirty years ago, 360-degree feedback surveys were very different than they are today. They were called "assessment instruments" and were designed exclusively for higher levels of management. They were called instruments because the early 360-degree feedback tools were modeled after psychological tests. They had a rigid set of items that the publishers claimed had been researched to correlate to several "constructs" or factors of leadership. The value of the feedback was based on the quality of the research. Processing the feedback was done off-site. You had to scan paper forms, check them, and send them to a central processing facility. The service was very expensive.

At my company, we took an outside-the-box approach to this technology. We felt that 360-degree feedback was so useful that everyone in the organization should be able to benefit from it, not just top management. That meant it had to be much less expensive to administer. We also felt that a rigid set of survey questions didn't make sense. Battalion commanders simply don't lead the same way that sales managers do. Ministers lead their congregations much differently than project managers lead their teams. In other words, an assessment needs to be customized locally to fit the culture.

So, we developed a new approach. We created a user-friendly PC-based system that an organization could purchase, customize, and administer locally. This meant that scanners were no longer needed, which cut the cost of administration dramatically. The software came with a huge library of generic skill/behavior sets that allowed easy, do-it-yourself customization so organizations could align surveys with their local competencies. The concept of researched constructs in a rigid instrument became an outmoded approach. The purpose of 360-degree feedback was to tell someone what coworkers thought about their work behavior so the recipient could decide whether to work on improving a given area—not to measure "traits," as in psychological testing.

This was an entirely new approach to 360-degree feedback. We believed it made more sense and would lead to a much wider use of performance feedback, which would be a boon to learning and development. And in the end, our vision proved to be the way of the future. While a few of these expensive old-style "instruments" continued to exist, they aren't used much anymore. Today, there are nearly 100 different feedback survey services on the market, all designed following our model.

But back in 1994, it was amazingly difficult to talk about this approach to Human Resource Development professionals. Our approach to feedback was so new that it conflicted with how they thought about it. Their mindset about feedback was conditioned by the old paradigm. They would say, "Show me your research." And we would answer, "This isn't a psychological test.

The question of validity is different. No survey can be valid for every organization. The questions are used to give feedback about individual behaviors, not to create constructs. The questions are based on a thorough search of the literature. To make them valid, we make it easy for users to customize them based on how their unique organization operates."

To understand the value of this new approach, learning and development professionals would have to open their minds to a new way of thinking. A few were able to do this right away. They became customers. For others, it took longer. Many were never able to grasp the new concept. They continued to pay ten times as much for feedback that was limited in its usefulness.

But that was a long time ago. The new paradigm is now the old paradigm.

It isn't easy to consider new ways of thinking. What about your old way of thinking? It's a part of who you are. You've had it in your brain for a long time, and so by now, it's interconnected with lots of other concepts. Letting a new notion in and making a home for it next to everything else you know takes work. That's why open-mindedness is considered a character skill.

But it's worth the effort. The reward is more insights and wisdom, which will help you make better decisions. It also means more creativity—new ideas, solutions, and possibilities. The world is changing all the time, and if you keep a closed mind, you won't be able to adapt to it.

When someone comes at you with a new thought and you feel that familiar discomfort, you'll be tempted to argue, to justify your own way of thinking, and prove the person wrong. I strongly urge you not to give in to that feeling.

Instead, say this: "Oh? That sounds interesting. Tell me more." You don't have to agree; you don't have to accept it as valid. Just give it a hearing. "How did you come to that conclusion?" Find out what the new thought is based on, analyze it logically, and consider whether it can be improved. If the notion has promise, you can consider whether it's worth the effort to build on it.

What is OPEN-MINDEDNESS?

Open-mindedness is the willingness to consider new ideas, perspectives, and information without being unduly influenced by preconceived notions, biases, or prejudices. You thoughtfully listen to different viewpoints and remain open to exploring ideas and possibilities you haven't considered before, even if they challenge your own beliefs and assumptions. You engage in thoughtful dialogue with a genuine desire to learn, understand, and grow rather than seeking to impose your views on others.

Why open-mindedness is important:

Everyone comes to work with different backgrounds and know-how. Everyone has a unique capacity for thought and creativity. The overriding principle: *You don't know everything. You don't have all the answers.* When people offer suggestions, you have nothing to lose by considering the input of the people around you. You don't have to agree with everything you hear, but if you hear people out, you may discover possible solutions you haven't considered before, and those could lead to significant success.

"If you keep thinking what you've always thought, you'll keep getting what you've always got."

Harvey Mackay, American author

What you can do to strengthen your open-mindedness:

- ✓ Learn more about diverse cultural practices, customs, and traditions.

- ✓ When engaging in debates or discussions, listen to understand opposing viewpoints and alternative arguments, even if you disagree.
- ✓ Actively seek new experiences and opportunities for learning.
- ✓ Routinely ask for input from others. Consider multiple options, weigh different perspectives, and avoid making hasty judgments.
- ✓ Show interest in the opinions, feelings, and experiences of others, even if they differ from your own.
- ✓ Explore new subjects or disciplines.
- ✓ When someone says something you disagree with, ask them how they came to their opinion.
- ✓ When someone suggests a faulty idea, first tell them what you like about it, then express your concerns. Ask them how you might overcome the concerns together.

Remember that open-mindedness is a behavior pattern. The more you put it into practice, the stronger it will get. Along the way, you can expect both successes and disappointments. So partner with someone to coach you with encouragement; then learn from your attempts, stick with it, and you'll get stronger over time.

"It ain't what you don't know that gets you into trouble. It's what you know for sure that just ain't so."

Mark Twain, American novelist

The wiser you are, the more you'll seek the wisdom of others.

"Adapt or perish, now as ever, is Nature's inexorable imperative."

H. G. Wells, British novelist

"The art of life is a constant readjustment to our surroundings."

Okakura Kakuzo, Japanese scholar

"Notice that the stiffest tree is most easily cracked, while the bamboo or willow survives by bending with the wind."

Bruce Lee, Chinese actor

"Only in growth, reform and change, paradoxically enough, is true security to be found."

Anne Morrow Lindbergh, American author

36

Flexibility

Adapt, and you will survive and thrive.

Once upon a time, a chemist invented a capsule that he claimed had all the nutrients for growing practically any kind of crop. All you had to do was plant it with the seeds, and it would slowly release the nutrients over time, establishing the ideal environment for growth.

Farmers saw that the little golden capsules worked, and the chemist prospered.

But as the growing seasons came and went, the chemist noticed some disturbing practices. Many of the farmers believed that the capsule had magical properties and would promote growth under any conditions. So, they stopped irrigating and tending the fields. Others believed that one usage of the capsule would last for years, maybe forever. Farming would become a leisurely pursuit, not the risky, laborious process it had always been.

The chemist pleaded with them to use common sense, but most of them preferred to believe that the capsules were "the answer."

Of course, the chemist's product wasn't magical, and as farmers failed to follow through, crops were lost. When that happened, they blamed the chemist for their misery. His capsules weren't the amazing solution to farming they had hoped for.

As his profits declined, the chemist made a crucial decision. Instead of improving his pill, he changed his business model altogether. He decided to create a different kind of nutrient system, one that would be used continuously throughout the normal cycle of agriculture. Creating something brand new meant going back to the drawing board, but eventually, he delivered a system that farmers would use throughout the growing season. His new product caused the farmers to pay attention to the realities of agriculture while giving them new tools and new methods. In the end, everyone prospered.

The moral of the fable? How about a cool proverb:

"No matter how far you have gone on a wrong road, turn back."

Turkish proverb

The fable of the chemist parallels the experience of my company.

In the previous chapter, I recounted how, back in 1992, we learned about a new computer service called 360-degree feedback. It collected and consolidated ratings and comments to give managers highly valid feedback about their leadership. For many managers, it provided a much-needed "wake-up call" to improve.

Unfortunately, the process was administratively cumbersome. Forms had to be filled out, collected, checked, scanned, and sent to a central processing facility. Besides being a bother, this made the service so expensive that most organizations used it only with executives. But if this kind of feedback was so valuable, managers at all levels needed it. The truth is that *all* employees needed it, even though it was impractical to offer it to them because the surveys themselves focused exclusively on high-level leadership. Another limitation was that they weren't easily customized to align them with the unique practices of an organization.

So, my company developed a radically new approach to 360-degree feedback. It put easily customizable survey software in the hands of the organization itself, reducing costs by an order of magnitude and making this kind of feedback practical for anyone in any organization. The program was so flexible that it could be used for all sorts of surveys, not just individual performance feedback.

In the end, it revolutionized 360-degree feedback technology, and before long, dozens of similar feedback tools began to appear on the market.

But there's more to this story. Like the chemist, we noticed that many organizations used 360-degree feedback inappropriately.

For one thing, instead of using it to diagnose the need for learning and development, some began to use it for annual performance reviews. We cautioned managers not to do this, but the temptation of using 360 to replace their flawed appraisal systems was too great. Unfortunately, when linked to personnel decisions, the feedback becomes subjective and politicized, making managers wary of the process.

Also, many organizations believed that one application of feedback would be enough to stimulate managers to improve their performance. Consequently, they didn't follow up with skill-building programs, and even fewer followed up with coaching and more feedback. So, when managers failed to change their behavior, they questioned the power of the feedback.

Although our company has a huge stock of know-how in this industry, instead of trying to build an even better feedback mousetrap, we decided to change our business model. We saw that the greater opportunity was to solve the real problem—the lack of on-the-job application. If we could create systems that facilitated developmental follow-through, organizations would be far more successful in their efforts to change behavior and improve performance.

So, we created an online learning program focused on practice and virtual coaching. It combined fresh multimedia content, exercises, and peer coaching to reinforce skills and character skills.

Changing course like this wasn't easy. I often joked that it was like leaning against a battleship. But everyone in the company pushed hard to be flexible with new goals, new roles, new tools, and new ideas. We leaned against the battleship together, and it moved our company in a new direction.

What is FLEXIBILITY?

Flexibility is the ability to adapt, adjust, or change in response to new circumstances. You're open to alternative approaches, ideas, or perspectives and are willing to modify your plans to get a better result. You embrace change, uncertainty, or ambiguity without becoming rigid or resistant. As a result, you're versatile and able to thrive in dynamic environments. You handle unexpected obstacles, pivot when necessary, and maintain a positive attitude and resilience in the face of unforeseen challenges.

Why flexibility is important:

It's not easy to recognize a legitimate need to change course. And if you do, this could mean seeking unfamiliar solutions and changing plans that have been heavily resourced. If people have bought into the status quo, their initial impulse may be to resist change, even if trying something different is a good idea. To them, keeping things the way they are may seem like the easiest solution. But if you and others aren't flexible enough to adapt to change, your organization could fail.

"Stay committed to your decisions, but stay flexible in your approach."

Anthony Robbins, American author

What you can do to strengthen your flexibility:

- ✓ Approach a tough problem from different angles, considering new ideas and ways to adjust your approach.
- ✓ If you should feel the need for a career change, explore new industries or roles. If necessary, acquire new skills related to the new professional path.
- ✓ Ask people for their ideas, perspectives, and feedback.
- ✓ Be flexible in the way you face changes in organizational policies, processes, or technology.
- ✓ In your relationships, work to achieve win-win solutions, considering other opinions and adjusting expectations to maintain harmony.
- ✓ Faced with unexpected events, change your daily routine, reprioritize tasks, and reallocate time.
- ✓ When reacting to change, favor approaches that can improve your situation.
- ✓ No new idea is all good or all bad. When someone proposes a change, before you voice your concerns, tell them what you like about the idea. Then suggest a build on the idea or a couple of other creative approaches.

Flexibility is a behavior pattern. The more you react to change with new directions, the stronger your pattern will get. So, partner with people who are willing to discuss your ideas with you. What you need is someone to encourage you as you try to adapt to change. Don't give up, and you'll become consistently more successful over time.

"Enjoying success requires the ability to adapt. Only by being open to change will you have a true opportunity to get the most from your talent."

Nolan Ryan, American professional baseball player

Change as conditions change, and you won't be left behind.

Conclusion

As you examine some of the chapters of this book, you'll see that it's possible to become stronger and more effective in many important ways. You can become much more successful in your life, relationships, and work. Growing stronger as a person can involve a journey of lifelong personal development.

You'll need to commit to working on it: "getting your reps" by applying a skill often in your life and work. If you do, your brain will wire itself for the behavior pattern, and it will become a part of who you are.

This process of establishing permanent behavior patterns takes effort and inevitably has its ups and downs. Often, your practice will go very well, and you'll feel gratified. Other times it won't, and you might feel discouraged.

To stick with it, I strongly recommend that you partner with someone who cares about your success and will discuss your efforts with you and encourage you as you learn from them.

And while you're on this journey, refer back to the chapter about the skill you're working on. Having clarity about the how-to at your fingertips can help keep you on track.

Working on strong character is perhaps the most significant self-development you can undertake. So don't give up. The people around you need you to be successful.

Support Tools for You

For more than 30 years, our software company, Grow Strong Leaders (GSL), has created learning technologies that strengthen leader and team communication skills.

ASSESSMENT:

GSL 360—A 360-degree feedback platform that makes it easy to gather feedback about individual strengths and prioritize individual development.

- Extensive Survey Library with behavior-based surveys for:
  - 10 Communication Skills
  - 36 Character Skills
  - Executive Leadership (senior-level executives)
  - Team Leadership (supervisors and managers)
  - Personal Leadership (individual contributors)
- Recommended actions and resources for development
- Easy-to-read reports

DEVELOPMENT:

Online subscription programs that support ongoing accountability, reinforcement, and encouragement to build strong leader and team communication skills and character skills.

GSL PowerPartners—Participants form peer coaching partnerships to build communication skills using the books, ***Connect with Your Team*** and ***Peer Coaching Made Simple***, supported by 45 videos. Each video features tips that guide learners to improve one of these 10 skills:

- Listen to understand
- Coach people to think
- Guide learning from experience
- Get buy-in for expectations
- Offer encouragement
- Express appreciation
- Give feedback constructively
- Accept feedback graciously
- Engage in dialogue
- Resolve conflict creatively

GSL SkillBuilder—This powerful coaching support platform will transform the way you help leaders develop their communication skills and character skills with the support of a coach. The two books and 45 videos above are included, as well as this book and a wealth of resources and exercises for developing 36 areas of character strength, including integrity, composure, perseverance, and courage.

These two platforms will empower you to create a culture where managers and employees thrive.

About the Author

As CEO of Grow Strong Leaders, Dr. Coates has published articles, books, and online programs for workplace communication skills for over 30 years. These award-winning, brain-based assessment and learning programs have been used by millions of people worldwide. A graduate of West Point (1967), he retired from the U.S. Army as a lieutenant colonel (1987). He earned his Ph.D. from Duke University (1977) and has served on the faculties of the United States Military Academy, the Armed Forces Staff College, the College of William and Mary, and the Center for Creative Leadership.

www.ingramcontent.com/pod-product-compliance
Lightning Source LLC
LaVergne TN
LVHW020710110826
845149LV00012B/2196